The Real Rights of Man

The Real Rights of Man

Political Economies for the Working Class 1775–1850

Noel Thompson

Pluto  Press

LONDON • STERLING, VIRGINIA

First published 1998 by Pluto Press
345 Archway Road, London N6 5AA
and 22883 Quicksilver Drive, Sterling, VA 20166–2012, USA

British Library Cataloguing in Publication Data
A catalogue record for this book is available from the British Library

ISBN 0 7453 1270 5 hbk

Library of Congress Cataloging-in-Publication Data
Thompson, Noel W., 1951–
   The real rights of man : political economies for the working
class, 1775–1850 / Noel Thompson.
      p.   cm. — (Pluto critical history)
   Includes bibliographical references and index.
   ISBN 0–7453–1270–5 (hc.)
   1. Economics—Great Britain—History.   2. Socialism—Great
Britain—History.   3. Great Britain—Economic
conditions—1760–1860.   I. Title.   II. Series.
HB103.A2T55 1998
330'.0942—dc21   98–36082
                                                                        CIP

Designed and produced for Pluto Press by
Chase Production Services, Chadlington, OX7 3LN
Typeset from disk by Gawcott Typesetting Services
Printed in the EC by T.J. International, Padstow

Contents

Pluto Critical History Series

The contemporary world is wracked with disaster, largely man made. The triumphalism of the world's rulers in the 1980s for the victory of capitalism has given way in the 1990s to anxiety and self doubt in the face of the failures of the 'tiger economies', the ongoing crisis in the former Eastern bloc and the serial incidence of famine and brutal war in Africa. Clearly the market offers no solution to the problems of the overwhelming majority of people on the planet. It has become increasingly urgent to understand the roots of the present crisis as a vital component in creating the agencies for the massive change essential to the permanent improvement of the condition of human beings in the century ahead.

Pluto Critical History aims to make a modest, though important, contribution to this process by providing a series of lively, accessible and original texts which will uncover, analyse and interpret themes and episodes in the past. It is determinedly non-sectarian socialist and internationalist in its pitch, enthusiastically encouraging new writers and aiming to assist understanding for students at all levels pursuing formal courses, as well as the critical general reader who simply 'wants to know'.

John Charlton
Series Editor

Preface

In 1793 a London seller of radical books and tracts, Thomas Spence, published a pamphlet entitled *The Real Rights of Man*. The title was deliberately chosen to signal the difference between his view of how best to emancipate those whom Burke had termed the 'swinish multitude' and that advanced in Tom Paine's *Rights of Man*, 1791. For Spence, Paine had failed to grasp that the real rights of man must be grounded in the possession of economic power. Without that, mere political rights were devoid of significance, and demands for liberty, equality and fraternity so much empty rhetoric. Securing the rights of man as conceived by Paine would do nothing to protect the multitude from the exactions and oppression of those who had the capacity to grant or deny access to the means of producing and thence to the means of life itself. For Spence, 'the question is ... no longer about what form of government is most favourable to liberty ... but which system of society is most favourable to existence and capable of delivering us from the deadly mischief of great accumulations of wealth which enables a few unfeeling monsters to starve whole nations'.[1]

This book is primarily concerned with those who, like Spence, prioritised the economic and who believed that only when labour ceased to be economically impotent would its emancipation from impoverishment and subjugation become possible.[2] It discusses the work of those agrarian radical, anti-capitalist and socialist writers who, in late eighteenth- and early nineteenth-century Britain, sought to formulate political economies for the working class which would both analyse the causes of their powerlessness and destitution and point to the manner and the means by which they might secure their real, economic rights.

As this book makes clear, the ways in which they believed this task could be accomplished were many and varied. What we have, indeed, is a plurality of political economies as writers attempted to come to terms with an unparalleled transformation of a primarily agrarian economy into one which, by 1850, possessed most of the hallmarks of a complex, urban, industrial economy. I have tried throughout, therefore, to make the reader aware of the shifting economic backdrop against which the work of these writers was set both to highlight some of the salient material realities which they sought to explain and to suggest how these did, in fact, impinge on and shape their respective political economies. Postmodernists may bridle at such methodological naiveté but, without trying to suggest an unproblematic relationship between economic language and economic circumstance, this writer none the less believes that an appreciation of the latter does allow a more nuanced reading of the former. Indeed, he would go further and suggest that a sensitive reading of political economies is impossible without a due understanding of the relevant period of economic history.

I have tried, wherever possible, to let those whose writings I have discussed speak for themselves and I have limited references to other works to a bare minimum. However, in the Further Reading section I have indicated not only the key primary but also important secondary texts which the reader may usefully consult. The list of the latter can also do service as an acknowledgement, on my part, to those whose thinking on anti-capitalist and socialist political economy has materially shaped my own. It is they, and the two decades of Swansea students persuaded by me to consider 'Economic Theory in Historical Perspective', who have engendered the enthusiasm I still have for the ideas of those who sought, during a pivotal period in British economic history, to furnish a political economy for the working class which articulated their experience, advanced their material interests and showed them how they might ultimately secure for themselves the real rights of man.

CHAPTER 1

Agrarian Radicalism: Thomas Spence and William Ogilvie

Throughout the eighteenth and well into the nineteenth centuries agriculture was the dominant sector of the British economy. Estimates suggest that, in 1801, agriculture accounted for 32.5 per cent of the Gross National Product and, in 1811, 35.7 per cent; the comparable figures for mining, manufacturing and building were 23.4 per cent and 20.7 per cent.[1] In 1801 35.9 per cent (1.7 million) of the British workforce were engaged in agriculture, forestry and fishing as against 29.7 per cent (1.4 million) in manufacturing and mining.[2] In addition it has been estimated that, in 1811, some 896,000 families were supported by agricultural occupations, some 35 per cent of the total.[3] Further, many of those involved in trade and manufacture also had a connection with the land, which often made a significant contribution to their livelihood, while rental income was, of course, an important source of investment for industrial activity.

So during the period when Thomas Spence and William Ogilvie penned their major works, the ownership of land was synonymous with economic and, inevitably, political power. As regards the latter, this clearly resided with a landed elite. Opinions might vary as to the size of that elite, the distribution of power within it and the extent to which it accommodated new arrivals, but there is no doubt that it dominated the institutions of central and local government and continued to do so well into the nineteenth century.[4] Writing of the 1760s, one commentator has stated that Parliament

> still bore the appearance of a gentlemen's club. The Lords remained in many respects the senior members: their small number evidence of their exclusivity; their rank, a testimony to their landed wealth; their influence over the membership of the Commons through their electoral strength growing rather than receding; their supervision of local administration, still immensely strong.[5]

As regards the distribution of economic power and the political influence that derived from land ownership, the phenomenon of enclosure should be particularly noted. It is true that, by 1760, at least 75 per cent of the land area of England and Monmouthshire had been enclosed and that there are good reasons for seeing 'the seventeenth rather than the eighteenth century as holding the pre-eminent position in the history of English enclosures'.[6] Nevertheless, the parliamentary enclosures of the late eighteenth and early nineteenth centuries affected over 7 million acres of open and common land. In the period 1750–1820 some 20.9 per cent of England was enclosed by Act of Parliament or, as a proportion of agricultural land, c. 30 per cent, and within that broad period, enclosure of open fields, common lands, meadows and waste was pursued with particular vigour in the 1760s and 1770s (900 Acts) and again 1793–1815 (2,000 Acts).[7] Without, in any way, minimising the importance of what occurred in the seventeenth century, therefore, it was still the case that, as one writer has put it, 'much of England was still open in 1700; but most of it was enclosed by 1840'.[8]

All this had a number of consequences, many of which have been a matter of intense debate among historians. But as regards the political economy of agrarian radicalism, the impact which enclosure had on the distribution of land ownership and the consequent distribution of the national income was of particular significance. As regards the former, it seems clear that there was, prior to and throughout the eighteenth century, a tendency for farms to be consolidated into larger and more efficient units, and this trend existed independently of enclosure. As Mingay has put it, 'the decline of small farms was not a new phenomenon resulting from parliamentary enclosures and more widespread adoption of improved techniques, but was the long-term effect of forces which had been at work well before the eighteenth century'.[9] Yet it was also the case that enclosure accelerated that trend and, in the view of some historians, did so markedly.

To begin with, many small landowners were bought out as a necessary preliminary to the enclosure process. Also the costs of enclosure spelt the demise of many. Thus 'small proprietors were … charged at a greater proportional rate for general expenses than were larger proprietors, and they were hit harder by the relative costs of fencing a small area being much more than for larger allotments'.[10] In addition, in terms of meeting expenses and paying the higher rents that followed enclosure, the larger landowners were better placed than smallholders and they were also better equipped to survive and prosper as agriculture became increasingly market-oriented.[11] Further, and most obviously, the loss of common rights meant that the holdings of small propri-etors were frequently no longer viable. Where rights could be established, land might be awarded by way of compensation but this was not always possible, and even where it was, there is evidence that the compensation was inadequate. As regards tenants, it was again the case that in a period of rising rents and shortening of leases circumstances militated in favour of the large rather than the small. Enclosure also 'provided landlords with an excellent opportunity of consolidating small farms into large ones which were easier to manage and meant less outlay on buildings and repairs' and the collection of rents.[12]

All this meant that 'after enclosure there were fewer small owner-occupiers and tenants, and more large tenants and landowners'.[13] Enclosure facilitated engrossing and the size of farms increased markedly in the late eighteenth century. In Leicestershire and Buckinghamshire, for example, it has been estimated that the fall in the number of original owners in enclosed parishes was 38 per cent in the period 1780–1820. More generally it has been suggested that by the turn of the century only some 15–20 per cent of the land was held by those who could be defined as smallholders.[14]

In terms of the distribution of national income all this contributed to a marked increase in rents. For landowners this was the *raison d'être* of enclosure. As Mingay has put it, 'the prime movers in enclosure were usually the larger proprietors ... their interest in it was largely a financial rather than an agricultural one. Landlords knew that enclosed farms yielded much higher rents.'[15] Certainly rents increased dramatically during the period of parliamentary enclosure. It is true they would have done so without enclosure. In the period 1750–90, for land unaffected by enclosure, the rise in rents was of the order of 40–50 per cent, but where land was enclosed 'a doubling to tripling of rents often followed ... In Lincolnshire and Wiltshire, for example, rents tripled.'[16] The rise in food prices which accompanied the Revolutionary and Napoleonic Wars also added a further twist to rental inflation. 'According to the Board of Agriculture the rise in rents between 1790 and 1813 was in the region of 84 per cent ... modern research has suggested that increases were commonly of the order of 90–100 per cent.'[17] It was indeed this rise of food prices that precipitated the wave of parliamentary enclosures in the period 1793–1815. The gains to be had from price rises and enclosure were therefore distributed disproportionately in favour of the enclosing landowners.

As both contemporaries and subsequent commentators have remarked, all this made for greater social tension and antagonism in landed society. What one sees, as E.L. Jones has put it, is a 'hardening three-way socio-economic division into landowners, tenant farmers, and hired labourers' as disparities in income between these 'divisions' increased during the Revolutionary and

Napoleonic Wars;[18] while, at same time, 'these [social] categories
gained ground at the expense of the smaller owner-occupiers and
the class of independant cottagers with enough miscellaneous
common rights, real or assumed, to have kept them largely out of
the labour market hitherto'.[19] Also, as regards this widening and
hardening of social divisions, an increasingly capitalised agriculture, where an adequate rate of return on what was invested was
an ever more powerful imperative, also involved changes in the
organisation of labour and work practices which engendered
resistance and social tension.[20]

   This growing social antagonism manifested itself throughout
the late eighteenth century in various forms of rural protest, many
directed at the process of enclosure; but it did so with particular
intensity during the war years over the issue of wages. Such
protests were, as one writer has put it, 'the first signs of the
growing strength of the agricultural proletariat, whose potential
was to be fully realised for the first time in East Anglia, 1815–16,
after the sudden removal of the wartime employment conditions'.
These 'Bread or Blood' riots involved social unrest on a scale
which was not seen again in agricultural areas until the Swing
riots of 1830–31.[21]

   It is against this backdrop that any consideration of the work of
Spence and Ogilvie must be set. For these writers recognised the
economic and political power that derived from the ownership of
land and saw in its increasing concentration the inevitable and
essential cause of the social and material evils which afflicted
labour.

   Born in Newcastle upon Tyne on 21 June 1750, Thomas
Spence was one of 19 children. His father was Jeremiah Spence,
a netmaker, originally from Aberdeen, and his mother, Margaret
Flet, was from Orkney. They were, as one commentator has put
it, 'among those poor Scots immigrants who largely populated
Sandgate, the Quayside ... the overcrowded home of waterside
workers, keelmen and labourers'.[22] Thomas Spence himself
referred to the hard struggle to subsist by honest effort and the
drudgery which characterised the lives of his parents and others
like them.

   Spence remained in Newcastle, supporting himself as a schoolmaster, until 1792 and this early part of his life clearly had a
profound influence on this thought. To begin with, during the
1760s and 1770s, Newcastle experienced an upsurge of radical
activity with a burgeoning of debating clubs and radical societies.
The Wilkesite agitation for parliamentary reform and the
Middlesex election of 1769, the American War of Independence,
the contested elections in Newcastle of 1774, 1777 and 1780 – all
played a part. Of singular importance, however, was the attempt,

in 1771, by the local landed elite, in the guise of the Mayor and Corporation of Newcastle, to enclose Newcastle Town Moor without the consent of the burgesses. The burgesses took successful legal action to prevent this and their success was followed by the passage of the Town Moor Act, 1774. This gave the burgesses the right to decide on the future leasing of land; such leasing being limited to 100 acres, for a term of seven years, with the rents which accrued being distributed to burgesses in reduced circumstances and their widows.[23] The significance of this event for Spencean political economy will be considered below, but at this point it is interesting to note that some 30 years later Spence was to remark: 'I took a lesson from this affair which I shall never forget ... the overbearing power of great men by their revenue.' Or, as a subsequent commentator has phrased it: 'the affair of the Moor clearly identified both the enemy and the source of his strength'.[24]

If such events had a profound influence, so too did the ideological milieu in which Spence moved during the period of his life that he spent in Newcastle. In this context, his association with the Reverend James Murray was of considerable importance. Spence's family attended Murray's Presbyterian chapel and it was through him that Spence was exposed to a number of ideas which, subsequently, were to loom large in his own thought. Specifically, there was Murray's emphasis on egalitarianism and democracy which are evident in, for example, his *New Sermons to Asses: Sermons to Doctors in Divinity*, 1771. Murray articulated a kind of biblical rationalism which used the Scriptures to establish the equality of all men in the sight of God and to enunciate their consequent equal claim to certain natural and inalienable rights. Almost inevitably such a position involved an antipathy to the enclosure of common land which was seen as depriving the poor of their 'common estate' and therefore of their most fundamental natural right – the right to the means of life.[25] Enclosure was, therefore, akin to theft and murder; it paved the way for the oppression of the poor. As he phrased it in *New Sermons*, 'the claims of freedom and liberty ended with the division of the common' and in consequence, he believed that the size of landed properties and rented farms should be restricted.[26] Further, in *The Contest*, 1774, an account of the dispute over the attempted Town Moor enclosure, he looked to a situation where the rents accruing to the burgesses from the leasing of common land would be applied 'to the widening of our narrow streets – the supplying of the town with plenty of soft, palatable water – the support of the poor; or encouraging new branches of trade and manufactures'.[27] Thus Murray clearly envisaged the possibility of using a rental surplus for collective purposes sanctioned by local government.

Here Murray's emphasis on the decentralisation of power and democracy should also be noted. On matters ecclesiastical, 'Murray preached and practised the fullest congregational independency.' Both Presbytery and Episcopacy were to be condemned as involving ecclesiastical tyranny and corruption. Only with congregational autonomy and democracy could the purity of the Primitive Apostolic Church be restored and Murray looked forward, in millennial fashion, to a time 'when all dominion shall be put down and God shall be all in all'.[28]

Egalitarianism, the communal use of surplus wealth, the decentralisation of economic and political power and the prospect of a sudden, transformative, sweeping away of existing ills and evils – these were to be central themes in the writing of Thomas Spence. It is also interesting to note here that after his move to London in 1792 Spence reprinted part of Murray's *Fast Day Sermons* in *Pig's Meat*, a three-volume miscellany of excerpts from the works of political writers, which Spence published in weekly penny parts over the period 1793–95.[29]

However, in addition to James Murray, two other influences should be noted. First, there is James Harrington, the author whose work was most often reproduced in *Pig's Meat*. Harrington's *Oceana* was cited at length, while Spence also quoted a long extract from Harrington on the freedom of the press during his trial for criminal libel in 1801. From Harrington, Spence seems to have derived in particular the idea, fundamental to his political economy, that the distribution of landed property determined the distribution of political power and thence the nature of the political system. From Harrington too came the notion that revolutions were necessary to restore the balance of interests in a state where these had become skewed in such a way as to threaten tyranny. Harrington's was also an influence which would have engendered a mistrust of central government which, as we shall see, was a salient characteristic of Spence's thought.[30]

Second, there is the Bible, a close familiarity with which would have been a consequence of Spence's religious upbringing. Certainly Spence's writing is permeated by biblical imagery and a chiliastic rhetoric with which he sought to evoke the swift and profound nature of the tranformation which he sought. Further, as regards the substance of that change, it is clear that Spence derived inspiration from the Old Testament and, in particular, the Mosaic agrarian law articulated in Chapter 25 of Leviticus.

Spence first aired his views on political economy before the Newcastle Philosophical Society on 8 November 1775. According to Allen Davenport, an early biographer of Spence, the title of the lecture was *On the Mode of Administering the Landed Estate of the Nation as a Joint Stock Property in Parochial*

Partnerships by Dividing Rent, a title that provides an accurate summary of the essence of what was subsequently labelled Spence's Plan. *Pig's Meat* alludes to its publication as *The Poor Man's Advocate* in Newcastle in 1779. However, the first extant published edition of the lecture is that of 1793, when it appeared under the title of *The Real Rights of Man*.[31]

For Spence, 'the country of any people, in a native state, is properly their common, in which each of them has an equal property, with free liberty to sustain himself and family with animals, fruits and other products thereof'. The emergence of private property in land was, therefore, a fundamental departure from this natural order of things and resulted 'either [from] ... conquest or encroachment on the Common Property of Mankind'. As to those who subsequently acquired land by purchase, they were simply accomplices to the original crime. 'Modern purchasers are not ignorant of the manner in which landed property was originally obtained ... everyone knows that buying stolen goods is as bad as stealing.'[32]

The right to an equal property in land was a natural right because it conferred the means to subsist and, therefore, was synonymous with the right to life itself. 'There is no living but on land and its productions,' wrote Spence, 'consequently what we cannot live without, we have the same property in as in our lives'. In addition, land was 'ours by right of policy, because, by the aid of it, and the revenues it produces the owners are enabled to rule over us, starve us, or do with us what they please'. Thus throughout Spence's writing there was a clear recognition that land is power – 'all dominion is rooted and grounded in land'.[33] Without the economic power that land conferred, oppression, or vulnerability to oppression, was clearly inevitable. Thus landowners, 'by granting the means of life', believed they granted 'life itself, and of course they [thought] they ha[d] a right to all the services and advantages that the life or death of the creature they [give] life to [can] yield'. Further, where private land ownership existed, the landowning interest would determine the formulation of national policy, ensuring that it advanced their interests. For it is, as Spence put it, 'natural to expect that whether in the legislature or out of it, their whole study will be, under every kind of government, to increase the price of what their estates produce, that their rents may rise'.[34]

Here Spence contrasted his position with that of the political radicals of the period and, in particular, that of Paine.[35] Paine might discourse on 'the rights of man', but those rights lacked substance unless underpinned by a system of landholding that invested individuals with the power to make them effective. It was that, and not the form of government, which would determine the freedoms that could be enjoyed and the rights that could be exercised. 'Search history', he wrote, 'and see that the government of every country ever was, and is, in the proprietors of land. If then the people wish to have the government of the country in their own hands, they must begin first by taking the land into their own hands.'[36]

Throughout his political economy Spence stressed the primacy of economic over political power. The distribution of the former determined who would wield the latter. This is what the French revolutionaries and their sympathisers in Britain had neglected. Their revolution had stopped short. It had not been extended into the economic sphere.

> And during the propagation of the true system certain philosophers shall arise of great abilities who shall erect a false Tree of Liberty ... they shall so animate the people with their display of the specious, but partial Rights of Man, that the multitude shall arise and great convulsions shall be in many countries ... and governments shall be overthrown, but oppression shall still remain.

'What does it signify whether the form of a government be monarchical or republican while estates can be acquired? ... while estates can be either purchased or acquired in any manner all governments will be rapacious and traitorous, and all men villains.' Where, however, the land became again as once it had been, the people's common, in which each had an equal property, then real democracy and liberty would follow as a matter of course. For 'citizens being thus kept on a[n] [economic] level without superiors, universal suffrage follows of course as well as universal capability of being elected'.[37] From its origins, therefore, socialist political economy in Britain acknowledged the determining role of the economic and, in looking to transform existing social and political arrangements, sought to alter, fundamentally, the distribution of economic power.

Further, with Newcastle Town Moor clearly in mind, Spence considered that the material and political evils resulting from the skewed distribution of land ownership had been compounded in the late eighteenth century by parliamentary enclosure. 'Great landlords and great farmers, now engross the country' enhancing the power of the 'host of hereditary Tyrants and Oppressors', proletarianising those whose independence had previously depended on common rights, widening social divisions and ensuring that the resultant expansion of output flowed into the hands of the large landowners in the form of increased rents.[38] On all these points Spence was both explicit and clear. Of the commoditisation of labour and the redistributive consequences, Spence wrote that when

> our rich neighbours took it into their heads to enclose our common. Then it was that you and I and many more poor people found a great alteration. We could neither keep cow, nor sheep, nor geese as before. Everything now depended on the ready penny and to crown our misery every opportunity was taken to raise our rents and lower our wages.

As to the distribution of the advantages which derived from enclosure, Spence noted:

> in defence of dividing commons it is alleged that land in a state of enclosure and tillage is of more advantage to the community at large. Very true; it is so. But why should the poor alone be robbed for the public good? If the welfare of the community require tillage and enclosure, let those who have the right to the common share the rent of the same when it is enclosed.[39]

Thus, unlike many of the critics of enclosure, Spence accepted that productivity gains might eventuate and output expand, but he also raised the fundamental question of what should be done where public benefit entailed private loss; a question all the more pressing, as he recognised, when the loss was suffered by those least able to bear it and the public benefit accrued disproportionately to the rich. It is interesting to note here that a subsequent generation of socialist writers was, in a comparable manner, to raise the same kind of question with respect to mechanisation and other productivity-raising developments set in train by industrialisation.

What then was to be done to restore to the people their natural rights; to undermine the power of the monopolisers and engrossers of land; to destroy the economic foundations of political tyranny; to lay those of a truly democratic polity and to ensure a fair distribution of that surplus which labour alone created? 'A day', wrote Spence, should be

> appointed on which the inhabitants of each parish meet, in their respective parishes, to take their long-lost rights into possession, and to form themselves into corporations ... The land, with all that appertains to it, is in every parish, made the property of the corporation or parish, with as ample power to let, repair, or alter all, or any part thereof as a Lord of the Manor enjoys.[40]

Thus what Spence advocated was the parochialisation and not, as some commentators have suggested, the nationalisation of land. Whether Spence envisaged that this would be peacefully effected or otherwise is something that has provoked considerable debate. However, it seems clear, particularly as the 1790s progressed, and as the government showed itself increasingly willing to resort to coercion to suppress dissent, that Spence, while hoping for a non-violent transference of ownership, both contemplated and accepted the use of force. Thus in the *Rights of Infants* he warned existing landowners that 'if, by foolish and wicked opposition, you should compel us in our own defence, to confiscate even your moveables, and perhaps also to cut you off, then let your blood be on your own heads, for we shall be guiltless'. Elsewhere he was adamant that 'when the government violates the rights of the people, insurrection becomes to the people ... the most sacred and most indispensable of duties'.[41]

The land, once in parochial ownership, would be leased to those who constituted the parish, on such a basis as to ensure that all who so desired would have the opportunity to engage in agriculture. The result would be a proliferation of small farmers and thence an end to those disparities of wealth and power which had previously made for oppression and exploitation. Thus, 'we may suppose that farms would be so small, that the farmers would hardly be rich enough to hoard much, neither would they be so few in number as easily to combine to raise the price of their produce'.[42]

The rental surplus previously appropriated by large landowners would now be retained by the parish and used to pay the national

> government its share of the sum which the parliament or national congress at any time grants; in maintaining and relieving its own poor, and people out of work; in paying the necessary officers their salaries; in building, repairing and adorning its houses, bridges and other structures; in making and maintaining convenient and delightful streets, highways and passages both for foot and carriages; in making and main-taining canals and other conveniences for trade and navigation, implanting and taking in waste grounds; in providing and keeping up a magazine of ammunition, and all sorts of arms sufficient for all its inhabitants in case of danger from enemies; in premiums for the encouragement of agriculture, or anything else thought worthy of encouragement.

Rent would, in effect, become truly a social surplus to be used for social purposes and, specifically, on parochial initiative, to upgrade the nation's social and economic infrastructure.[43]

To ensure the perpetuance of this state of affairs, land would cease to be a marketable commodity. 'The power of alienating the least morsel, in any manner, from the parish, either at this or any time hereafter is denied.' The possibility of any future concentration of land ownership and thence power would, therefore, have been removed. The basis would have been laid, both locally and nationally, for a permanent decentralisation of economic and political power.[44]

Spence also envisaged such a transformation of land ownership as producing structural changes in the economy. He anticipated that with the breaking-up of 'over-large farms' and the multiplication of small tenant farmers there would be a consequent 'wholesome decrease of artificers and tradesmen, who are now out of all proportion too numerous'.[45] And this, together with his emphasis on the primacy of land as regards the distribution of economic and political power, has led some commentators to suggest that Spence articulated a socialist political economy that took little account of contemporary economic developments and was therefore destined to be rapidly rendered redundant as industrialisation gathered momentum and the locus of economic power shifted from the land. In this view of things Spence's Plan was 'no more than the traditional dream of a local society of good husbandmen and moral economy' and he 'had little grasp of the economic realities of the late eighteenth century ... concentrat[ing] all his attention on the agricultural sector of the economy just at a time when Britain was undergoing rapid commercial and industrial development'.[46]

However, such criticisms are certainly misplaced. To begin with Spence's whole stress on land ownership as holding the key to social transformation was legitimate given the context in which he wrote. Agriculture's primacy in the economy and the extent to which the political system was dominated by the landed interest has already been remarked upon, and one might note too that recent research has emphasised the slow pace and embryonic nature of the commercial and industrial transformation which Britain was undergoing in this period. In any case Spence did not ignore the contribution which industry and commerce could make. Thus he looked not to the reconstitution of an agrarian past but to an economy where commerce and manufacturing played a significant role. This is clear from his imaginative descriptions of the 'Spensonia' which would emerge after his Plan had been put into effect. Thus its capital was seen as 'full of superb and well furnished shops and has every appearance of grandeur, opulence and convenience, one can conceive to be in a large place flourishing with trade and manufactures'.[47] What Spence gives us, therefore, is not so much a pastoral idyll as an idealised Newcastle.

What Spence believed was that trade and industry had been unnaturally expanded as a result of the existing pattern of land ownership. Many were forced into commerce and manufacturing because the option of husbandry was not open to them. With the institution of the Plan, however, 'trade will then be genuine, unforced and natural. For none will be in trade and manufactures, but those who can live well by them, because tillage would then be open to all in the case of difficulty.'[48] What he envisaged, therefore, was the emergence of a natural balance between commerce, industry and agriculture, one that had been destroyed by the private appropriation of the people's common.

In addition, and most importantly, Spence's vision of the socialisation of the means of production does not neglect the new sources of economic power which were emerging in the late eighteenth and early nineteenth centuries. It is true that Spence was relaxed as to the inequalities in the distribution of property which might emerge outside the agricultural sector. These he saw as largely legitimate, deriving, as he argued, from unequal effort:

> All men to land may lay an equal claim;
> But goods and gold unequal portions frame:
> The first because all men on land must live;
> The second's the reward industry ought to give.[49]

Further, he saw the inequalities in the distribution of non-landed property as relatively unimportant, in large part because its evanescent nature did not allow its owners to exert the kind of influence over the liberties of the population as those possessed of property in land. 'It is not worth regarding the trifling influence of moveable property alone on the liberties of the people; for when wealth cannot be rooted and fixed in land', wrote Spence, 'it is of a fluctuating and evaporating nature, and is apt, like the moisture of the earth, to take wings and fly away, unless restored by the showers of industry'.[50]

All that said, it is clear that, in addition to land, he anticipated that other productive means would be collectively owned. 'You know that all things which cannot be divided justly among a number of proprietors can yet be enjoyed with the nicest exactness in partnership. As for instance shipping, collieries, mines and many other great concerns. Partnership in trade is now well understood.' Elsewhere he wrote: 'the land and *buildings and other appurtenances*, should in every parish belong to ... the parishioners'. He also suggested a nationalisation of intellectual property rights, with all inventions to be purchased and exploited by the state.[51] In addition, and of particular importance in this context, Spence, in *A Description of Spensonia*, 1795, used the analogy of a voyage to illustrate the possibility of the formation of co-operative enterprises and to discuss the manner in which they might function. Here he clearly envisaged a form of socialist enterprise manifestly applicable to commercial and manufacturing activity.

Thus, using the analogy of a voyage, he has a 'father' address his 'sons' in the following terms:

> You shall all be equal owners and share the profits of every voyage equally among you. You shall choose from among yourselves one fit to be captain, another to be mate, another carpenter etc. – These officers shall continue in office while you please, and when you please you shall change them ... At the end of the voyage, or at other stated times agreed upon, you shall settle your accounts; and after paying the captain, the mate and every other officer and man his wages, according to station and agreement, and all bills for upholding wear and tear, provisions, &c., then the remainder, which is the net profit of the voyage ... is now your common property and must be shared equally amongst you all without respect to any office any one may have held. For as I make you all equal owners so shall you be equal sharers in the profits of each voyage.[52]

So the surplus generated by the activity of the co-operative enterprise was to be shared equally, even if the wages paid to the employees of the enterprise admitted of differentials. Such an arrangement, whatever its deficiencies, can certainly not be categorised as one that was inapplicable to an increasingly industrialised economy. What is remarkable, therefore, is not that Spence, writing when he did, gave primacy to the transference of land to public ownership, but that his vision of a socialist economy encompassed institutional arrangements applicable to commercial and industrial activity. This is perhaps less surprising when one notes that while, in the late eighteenth century, Newcastle was a town of little more than 30,000, it nevertheless represented 'a particularly striking example of the complex alliance of the landed interest with city merchants and large industries already run on capitalist lines'.[53] Dickinson has written that 'mines, factories and cotton mills had no place in Spence's vision of Britain's green and pleasant land',[54] but this ignores the fact that mines were most certainly accommodated, and, that factories were to remain, even for some time after Spence's death, an atypical form of industrial organisation. Further, the contribution of cotton mills to the Gross National Product was, in Spence's lifetime, dwarfed by that of agriculture.

Spence moved from Newcastle to London in 1792, where he established himself as a seller of radical books and pamphlets, his own included. The dissemination of such ideas, his involvement with the London Corresponding Society and the revolutionary Lambeth Loyalist Association,[55] together with the publication of radical broadsides and tracts, soon attracted the attentions of John Reeve's Association for the Preservation of Liberty and Property against Republicans and Levellers and those of the government. In consequence Spence was subjected to a campaign of legal and physical harassment. In December 1792 he was arrested and committed to prison for selling the second part of the *Rights of Man*; in 1794 he was imprisoned for seven months without trial and then, in 1801, convicted for seditious libel and imprisoned for twelve months for the publication of the *Restorer of Society to its Natural State*.

Such persecution suggests influence and, indeed, the Spenceans were mentioned by name in an Act of 1817, which made illegal certain 'societies or clubs' which 'hold and possess for their object the confiscation and division of the land'. A Society of Spencean Philanthropists was set up in 1816 soon after Spence's death,[56] and in the same year four leading members were tried for high treason after the Spa Fields Riots. Spenceans were also involved in the abortive Cato Street conspiracy of 1820. Important figures in post-war trade unionism such as Allen Davenport and John Gast were influenced by Spencean ideas. Discussion of the Spence's Plan appeared in radical papers such as *Cobbett's Political Register*, the *Black Dwarf* and the *Independent Whig*, while Home Office reports expatiated upon the widespread influence of Spenceanism. Coleridge and Southey, among others, noticed Spence's ideas[57] and an anonymous contemporary suggested that 'when Malthus published his *Essay on Rent* [1815], it seems to have been partly with a view to answer the cry of "no Landlords", which then stood rubric on the walls' – a clear reference to the contemporary practice of chalking 'Spence's Plan' on the walls of the capital.[58] In the 1820s and 1830s Spenceans played their part in the London Co-operative Society, the British Association for the Promotion of Co-operative Knowledge and the National Union of the Working Classes and, in general, the radical reformers of the 1830s numbered many, such as Bronterre O'Brien, upon whom Spenceanism had left its imprint.[59] Indeed figures such as O'Brien, Ernest Jones and George Harney can be seen as extending the influence of Spenceanism into the Chartist period.[60] Moreover when, in the 1880s and 1890s, the English Land Restoration League and the Land Nationalization Society once again generated popular support for the public ownership of land, they also made it their business to republish O'Brien's writings on the subject. Spenceanism can therefore be said to have remained part of the fabric of radical and socialist thinking throughout the whole of the nineteenth century. In this context it is difficult to understand G.D.H. Cole's remark that 'the writings of Thomas Spence ... had little practical bearing on the contemporary development of British radical or working-class thought'. Rather, one must agree with Chase that 'Spence's contribution to radical thought was one of substance, vitality and longevity.'[61]

As a number of commentators on Spence's thinking have pointed out, he was not alone in mooting the idea of a natural right to property in the earth, nor even in the advocacy of an agrarian law which would give some practical expression to this.[62] Thus, with William Ogilvie, we have another writer who, proceeding from premises very similar to Spence's, argued for a fundamental reform of the existing system of landholding. Ogilvie's *Essay on the Right of Property in Land* was published in 1782 and was probably read by Spence sometime in 1793. Certainly he draws attention to it in the second volume of *Pig's Meat*.[63]

William Ogilvie (1736–1813) was born near Elgin in the north of Scotland. The only son of the laird of Pittensear, he retained a practical interest in the land throughout his life but pursued an academic career which saw him become Professor of Humanity at the University of Aberdeen in 1765. Like Spence, he believed that 'the earth having been given to mankind in common occupancy, each individual seems to have by nature a right to possess and cultivate an equal share'. However, 'in the progress of commercial arts and refinement, it is suffered to fall into obscurity and neglect' and it was necessary, therefore, for measures to be implemented which would allow those who wished to do so to reclaim their 'birthright'.[64] Here, though, Ogilvie took on board the Lockean qualification that the mingling of labour with what nature had bestowed on all conferred a right to property in what resulted. There was a right to property by labour as well as the natural rights that derived from an original state of common occupancy. On the maintenance of the former right 'depended the perfection of the art of agriculture, and the improvement of the common stock and wealth of the community'; on the defence of the latter 'the freedom and prosperity of the lower ranks'. The problem was that 'in every country where agriculture has made considerable progress, these two rights are blended together, and that which has its origin in labour is suffered to eclipse the other founded in occupancy'.[65]

For justice to be done and the basis laid for continued agricultural progress it was necessary, therefore, to separate out these rights and bestow them on those to whom they should devolve. To this end Ogilvie distinguished three components of land value:

> the original value of the soil, or that which it might have borne in its natural state, prior to all cultivation ... the accessory or

improved value of the soil; that, to wit, which it has received
from the improvements and cultivation bestowed on it by the
last proprietor, and those who have preceded him ... The
contingent or improveable value; that further value which it
still may receive from future cultivation.[66]

As regards existing landowners, they should be 'allowed to have a
full and absolute right to the original, the improved, and contingent value of such a portion of [their] estate, as would fall to
[their] share, on an equal partition of the territory of the state
among the citizens'. However 'over all the surplus extent' of their
estates they would have a full right only to the 'accessory value'
whether bestowed by themselves or purchased from a previous
improver.[67]

What Ogilvie proposed, therefore, was the enactment of a
'Progressive Agrarian Law' by which citizens would be given the
opportunity to secure their natural right to land by 'claiming
from the public a certain portion, not exceeding forty acres, to
be assigned him in perpetuity'.[68] The creation of such 'standard
farms' was the ideal means of claiming the natural rights to
which a nation's citizenry were entitled. Yet at the same time
Ogilvie recognised the major obstacles in the way of implementing such a policy. Thus, he considered, it was 'only in
democratical governments of which there are very few, or in
unlimited monarchies during the reign of a sovereign endowed
with superior wisdom and capacity, that any sudden or effectual
reformation of the abuses of landed property can be expected',[69]
and Ogilvie was certainly not prepared to advocate either a
democratic revolution or an absolutist seizure of power to facilitate his programme of land reform. Rather, he believed it had
to be accepted that

> whatever inclination a wise and benevolent sovereign may have
> to communicate to all his subjects that prosperity which the
> reformation of property in land seems capable of diffusing, it
> may appear in most cases too hazardous for the public peace,
> and the security of his throne, to attempt the establishment of a
> wise equitable system at once, and in the whole extent of his
> dominions.[70]

In his *Essay*, therefore, Ogilvie rapidly moved from an articulation
of the ideal to a number of partial remedies, suggesting, for
example, that 'it might be expedient' to limit the creation of
standard farms 'to uncultivated lands alone, or to the forests and
demesnes of the crown, either of which would prove of great
public utility'. Further, he proposed that

the present method of dividing and enclosing commons, which, though favourable to cultivation, is known to curtail very much the independent rights and comfortable circumstances of the lower orders of the poor, be exchanged for some plan more allied in its aim to the provisions of the progressive Agrarian.[71]

So the objective was to move towards the ideal by expedients which did not immediately threaten existing property rights. In this respect Ogilvie differed markedly from Spence, even though their vision of an agricultural sector dominated by smallholders was remarkably similar. Also while, for Ogilvie, ownership would reside with the proprietor, for Spence, ownership was social and located in the parish.

What Spence and Ogilvie share is a visceral antipathy to the existence of large landowners. Thus while shying away from a direct challenge to the property rights which they exercised, Ogilvie none the less made clear in his *Essay* that he considered their 'exclusive right to the improveable value of the soil'

a most oppressive privilege by the operation of which the happiness of mankind has been for ages more invaded and restrained than by all the tyranny of kings, the imposture of priests, and the chicane of lawyers taken together, though these are supposed to be the greatest evils that afflict the societies of human kind.

Again, as with Spence, Ogilvie locates the primary cause of oppression in the coercive and exploitative use of economic power. Thus, 'it has been the oppression of the landholders and their agents, which has ever been the bane of Europe, more than even the oppression of the most arbitrary governments'.[72]

Further, the exaction of rents was subjected to a scathing attack in a manner redolent of Spence and, later, those radicals who drew their inspiration from Ricardo's onslaught on the income derived from the monopoly of a finite resource. In this regard 'the hereditary revenue of a great landholder' was seen as 'wholly independent of his industry ... It increases also without any effort of his, and in proportion to the industry of those who cultivate the soil.' This put the landowner on a par with 'a freebooter who has found means to cheat or to rob the public'. In words strongly reminiscent of those to be found in Ricardo's *Essay on the Profits of Corn*, 1815, Ogilvie was moved to write of the landowners that 'their interest is, in most important respects, directly opposite to the great body of the community, over whom they exercise an ill-regulated jurisdiction, together with an oppressive monopoly in the commerce of land to be hired for cultivation'.[73] Again, though, this radical critique of the economic role of the landowner eventuated in the suggestion of essentially ameliorative remedies, involving the fixing of rents, making leases perpetual or converting 'all farms into freeholds, with a reservation of the present rent to the landlord'.[74]

One final aspect of Ogilvie's political economy is worthy of note, one that was also to characterise the work of some later anti-capitalist and socialist writers, namely his belief in the economic and moral primacy of agriculture as a form of productive activity. To begin with, land represented the primary productive resource of any nation. Further – and here there are certainly parallels with Adam Smith's *Wealth of Nations* – Ogilvie argued that

> the labour of men applied to the cultivation of the earth tends more to increase the public wealth, for it is more productive of things necessary for the accommodation of life, wherein all real wealth consists ... and all labour applied to refined and commercial arts, while the state can furnish or procure opportunities of applying it to the cultivation of the soil, may be said to be squandered and misapplied.

Thus labour in the agricultural sector was viewed by Ogilvie as, almost invariably, more productive than that bestowed on other economic activities.[75] Further, such labour was 'most favourable to the virtue of the citizens ... Men employed in cultivating the soil, if suffered to enjoy a reasonable independence, and a just share of the produce of their toil, are of simpler manners, and more virtuous, honest dispositions, than any other class of men.'[76] Finally, as regards the nature of that productive activity, the industry of the agricultural labourer was 'not like that of the labouring manufacturer, insipidly uniform, but varied'. It obviated, therefore, that alienation and intellectual atrophy which Smith had identified as associated with the excessive subdivision of manufacturing activity.[77]

There are elements of all this too in Spencean political economy, but this theme of the economic and moral primacy of agriculture is much more fully developed in Ogilvie and is tied in more closely to a civic republican suspicion of luxury and 'the waste of great cities, of armies, navies, commercial and manufacturing occupations'.[78] However, as with Spence, Ogilvie believed that the optimum balance between agriculture and other forms of economic activity would follow on from the implementation of the agrarian reforms which he proposed. Where a citizenry could reclaim its birthright in the land, the 'balance' of the 'respective claims' of industry and agriculture would be 'adjusted in the most unexceptionable manner, by leaving men wholly to their free choice, and removing all obstruction and monopoly equally from the pursuit of both.'[79]

Beginning with the natural right of property in land, Ogilvie, therefore, proceeded to formulate a profoundly radical critique of the existing system and pattern of landholding. Both he and Spence identified land as the primary source of economic power; both aimed to alter its ownership and both recognised that this was a necessary prerequisite for any significant improvement in the material position of the bulk of the population. Both too relegated the political, as a cause of material evils, to a subsidiary position. It was also the case that, in most respects, they were inspired by a similar agrarian vision; an agricultural system where small landowners would dominate and where the greater part of the population would possess a measure of economic power, an interest in the improvement of the land and, therefore, in the material progress of society.

However Spence's ideal was to be realised through a revolutionary socialisation of landownership and among eighteenth-century agrarian radicals he was, *sui generis*, seeking as he did the total abolition of private property in land. In contrast Ogilvie's prescriptions were essentially reformist, taking as given the existing pattern of landownership and seeking to mitigate its worst excesses and worst consequences by facilitating the emergence of small independent proprietors. Also, for Ogilvie, only in the exceptional circumstances of democracy or absolutism was something more than incremental reform a possibility and he certainly did not advocate recourse to either political system. Spence thought in terms of a social revolution predicated on the collective ownership of the primary means of production. Ogilvie, even at his most radical, looked only to the social change that would eventuate from the multiplication of a virtuous and independent peasantry.

CHAPTER 2

William Cobbett and the Political Economy of 'Old Corruption'

The agrarian radicalism of Spence and Ogilvie directly addressed the economic plight of the labouring poor in an economy that was still predominantly agricultural. The political economy of 'Old Corruption' considered the material condition of labour in a period when that economy was experiencing the pressures of war. A number of radical writers contributed to its formulation, but by far the most important of these was William Cobbett. However, before considering Cobbett in his role as the implacable scourge of 'Old Corruption', it is necessary to confront him in a previous incarnation as the staunch defender of Tory England. For an appreciation of him in that guise is crucial to an understanding of the salient elements of the political economy he was subsequently to articulate.

It was as the tribune of Tory England that he deployed his considerable skills as a polemicist during a period which he spent in the United States in the 1790s and, for a short time, after his return to England in 1800. Using the pseudonym Peter Porcupine, he sought to rebut the scathing attacks on Britain and British foreign policy of the vituperatively pro-Jacobin democrats who dominated the American press. In doing so, he constructed an idealised British polity, against which both that of France and the United States could be matched and found wanting. In the spirit of Edmund Burke, Cobbett evoked the glories of a British Constitution which had emerged, slowly and organically, over many centuries in response to 'a thousand hidden causes, a thousand circumstances and unforeseen events'; a Constitution which had 'borne the test and attracted the admiration of ages'.[1] At the heart of that Constitution was the monarch; 'my sovereign, who, though his fleets command the ocean, though he is the arbiter of nations, and the acknowledged saviour of the civilised world, makes his chief glory consist in being the defender, the friend, *the father of his people*'.[2] The King was at the apex of a hierarchical but benevolently paternal polity and below him was a landed aristocracy, ancient in lineage and acting with a sense of both obligation towards the poor and respect for the rights of property. The essential beneficence of this polity was manifested in many ways but nowhere more clearly than in its treatment of the poor. Thus in response to a 'Charity sermon for poor emigrants', preached by the English radical Joseph Priestley in 1797, Cobbett wrote:

> the English system of poor relief [was] the best in the world; the fairest for the giver, and the least degrading for the receiver ... The poor man in England, *is as secure from beggary as is the king upon the throne.* The very worst that can befall him is to be obliged to make his distresses known to the parish officers, *to the heads of the great family of which he is a member,* who are obliged, by law, to give him what he needs, which he receives, not as alms, but as his legal due ... *that is the best country where poverty produces the least suffering of body and mind, and that country is Old England.*[3]

It was with such an ideal of Old England that Cobbett returned from the United States in 1800 to confront the realities of the new England that was being forged in the crucible of war with France. That conflict had dragged on with precious little sign of victory since 1793 and had, among other things, produced a substantial increase in public expenditure.

> By the second half of the 1790s when the French wars were well under way, net public expenditures were running at more than two and a half times their level in the corresponding quinquennium a decade previously. Even after deflating to allow for the price inflation which characterised this period ... net public expenditure in 1795/9 was averaging more than three times the 1770/4 level and twice the 1785/9 level.[4]

Further, between 1802 and 1815, gross public expenditure continued to rise rapidly from £65.5 million to £112.9 million.[5] This substantial expansion of public expenditure was financed primarily by an increase in government debt, but also by highly regressive indirect taxation, the former accounting for 27 per cent and the latter (excise duties and customs duties) for 44 per cent.[6] Thus over the period 1793–1814 the public debt rose from £242.9 million to £686.6 million with a comparable increase in the cost of debt servicing.[7]

In this financial milieu fortunes were to be made and unmerited income secured. The profits to be had from many wartime offices expanded apace. Those holding sinecures, where fees were paid on a scale determined by aggregate public expenditure or the volume of official business, benefited enormously, as both expanded rapidly during the war.[8] Faulty and inadequate

accounting and administrative systems made for waste and pecu-
lation. War contracts too allowed profits to grow in a manner
often unrelated to the goods and services actually furnished for
the war effort. The average rate of profits on these contracts at
between 10 and 20 per cent was not, in the words of one
commentator, 'scandalously high', but it was higher than the
9–14 per cent average rate of return which has been estimated for
investment as a whole. In addition, there were the costs incurred
and incomes to be secured from a burgeoning war bureaucracy,
which saw the number of government office holders increase from
16,267 in 1797 to 24,598 in 1815.[9]

In this context too prices rose, and rose rapidly. A price index
for 'domestic commodities' shows a rise from 91.6 in 1793 to
148.5 in 1814. Mokyr and Savin have suggested that there now
exists a consensus that the long-run price rise between 1788/92
and 1809/15 was of the order of 65–85 per cent. In addition,
during periods of harvest failure such as 1795/96 and
1799/1801, grain prices could rise to levels which precluded its
purchase by private households. Major outbreaks of food rioting
were a consequence.[10]

In contrast, and unsurprisingly, with prices rising so rapidly,
landowners also did well out of the war. They commanded the
crucial finite resource at a time when the military and civilian
demand for food was expanding rapidly, while the importation of
food was falling. Enclosure proceeded apace, indeed more swiftly
than at any other period in British history and, as noted above,
rents and rental income showed a marked increase. That said,
farmers do not seem to have benefited to a comparable extent. In
certain years high rates of return could be secured, but 'rates of
return on their capital above the customary level were short-
lived'.[11] Nevertheless, with agricultural prices rising in a buoyant
market, many were able to increase their absolute profits and, as
F.M.L. Thompson has written: 'one very general effect of the war
period was to engineer a considerable transfer of income from the
labouring and consuming sections to the agricultural community,
at least to the landowners and farmers, who were thus presented
with a sizeable unearned increment'.[12]

A massive expansion of public debt and a corresponding
increase in the burden of servicing it; a consequent rise in regressive taxation; an inflationary growth of the money supply as a
result of government efforts to finance the war; a burgeoning
bureaucracy and an associated augmentation in the numbers and
income of sinecurists and placemen supported by government
patronage; overall, a redistribution of income and wealth in
favour of enclosing landowners, the financial community, war
contractors and those able to seize the remunerative opportunities

which an expanded government service furnished – in the light of such developments it was inevitable that the Old England of Porcupine would come to look what it was: the figment of a febrile, polemical imagination. Thus a growing tension would emerge between the real and the Cobbettian ideal.

What served to heighten this tension was the conclusion, shortly after Cobbett's return to England, of the Peace of Amiens (1802) with France. Cobbett's journalism and pamphleteering in the United States had been primarily concerned with countering pro-French sentiment, keeping America neutral and, in that way, aiding the war effort. The Peace therefore represented an unseemly and contemptible capitulation to the regicide republic whose principles and practice he had damned. It was for Cobbett an 'improvident ... disgraceful ... heart-chilling ... courage-killing peace' and he progressed rapidly to a critique of the political system which had produced and embraced it.[13]

As Cobbett was increasingly to argue, the corrupt Peace was the product of a corrupt polity, a system debased by the expedients adopted to finance the war and to maintain in power those who prosecuted it. In Cobbett's ideal, 'Old England', an independent, natural aristocracy under the wise authority of a beneficent monarch, sought to manage disinterestedly the affairs of the nation. 'Now' (1802), however,

> the ancient nobility and gentry of the kingdom have, with a very few exceptions, been thrust out of all public employments: this part of the aristocracy has been, in some measure, banished from the councils of the state. A race of merchants, and manufacturers, and bankers and loan-jobbers, and contractors have usurped their place, and the government is very fast becoming what it must be expected to become in such hands.[14]

Herein lay the nature of the disease. The war and, especially, the means by which the war was financed, had elevated the commercial, manufacturing and financial interests at the expense of those who had been the guarantors of the liberties and privileges of Englishmen and the benefactors and protectors of the poor. A polity which had previously been held together by bonds of obligation and dependence was now governed according to the principles of financial gain. Those who wielded power no longer did so with an eye to duty and virtue but to self-interest and profit. In such circumstances, where 'a money-loving malady'[15] was rampant, the corruption of political and social life was a necessary consequence. It was this that lay at the root of labour's impoverishment, the suppression of freedoms and the venality of political life.

At the heart of 'Old Corruption', as Cobbett was to term it, was the 'Pitt System' of war finance. It was this that, *par excellence*, made possible the accumulation of fortunes unrelated to social pedigree or worth. It was this that had produced the social apotheosis of those moved by mercenary intent and the consequent baseness of policy-making. To understand 'The System' Cobbett consulted the work of George Chalmers and Adam Smith, but it was Tom Paine's *Decline of the English System of Finance* (1796, read in 1803), that made its machinations clear: 'Here was no bubble, no mud to obstruct my view: the stream was clear and strong: I saw the whole matter in its true light, and neither pamphleteers and speechmakers were, after that, able to raise a momentary puzzle in my mind.'[16]

Paine had argued that such was the accumulation of government debt engendered by the war and such the level of interest paid to service it, that compound interest would, with a predictable mathematical precision and certainty, effect the demise of the existing financial system and the polity with which it had become enmeshed. 'Who would have supposed', Paine had written, 'that falling systems ... admitted of a ratio apparently as true as the descent of falling bodies? I have not made the ratio any more than Newton made the ratio of gravitation.'[17] Cobbett adhered to such a view and was himself to make specific predictions as to the demise of 'The System', pointing to the suspension of cash payments by the Bank of England (1797) and the consequent growth of a 'paper money system' both as evidence of its decay and as developments which further compounded the malignant redistribution of wealth which the funding system was effecting. Thus the growth of a paper money system for Cobbett was synonymous with the growth in economic and social power of those financial interests that both printed that money and dealt in government debt. Further, Cobbett argued, the return to gold (cash payments) proposed by the Bullion Committee, 1810/11, would effect a savage deflation which would, at a stroke, substantially increase the real costs of servicing the National Debt and the real income of the holders of government stock. That such a measure was proposed and, in 1819, ultimately implemented, made only too clear once again the extent to which financial interests now determined and corrupted policy.

For Cobbett, therefore, the causes of labour's impoverishment and their link with Old Corruption were all too apparent. During the war, that impoverishment was the consequence of the increased taxes necessary to service an expanded and expanding National Debt, together with the price inflation that the increase in the volume of paper money had precipitated – wages, in such a context, failing to keep pace with the depreciation of the currency. In the aftermath of war, with the return to cash payments and the deflation that ensued, it was the substantial increase in the real burden of the National Debt and thence taxation which was at the root of labour's economic ills. 'Our present misery' was caused, wrote Cobbett, by

> the enormous amount of taxes, which the Government compels us to pay for the support of its army, its placemen, its pensioners ... and for the payment of the interest of its debt ... when we compare our present state to the state of the country previous to the wars against France, we must see that our present misery is owing to no other cause. The taxes then annually raised amounted to 15 millions: they amounted last year to 70 millions. The nation was then happy; it is now miserable.[18]

After the war, while Cobbett admitted that taxes had been reduced, this was only 'nominally'. In real terms, with price deflation, 'they have, in reality, been greatly augmented'.[19] It was this and this alone that explained the general economic depression, the mass unemployment and the wholesale immiseration which followed the war. 'Your distress', he wrote to the labouring classes,

> arises from want of employment with wages sufficient for your support. The want of such employment has arisen from the want of a sufficient demand for the goods you make. The want of a sufficient demand for the goods you make has arisen from the want of means in the nation at large to purchase your goods. This want of means to purchase your goods has arisen from the weight of taxes co-operating with the bubble of paper-money. The enormous burden of taxes and the bubble of paper money has arisen from the war, sinecures, the standing army, the loans, the stoppage of cash payments at the Bank.[20]

'What is the principal cause of that ruine and misery that now pervades the land and which makes the life of the industrious man hardly worth preserving?', asked Cobbett. His answer: 'the cause is the existence of a paper system by means of which the ... earnings of the industrious, are taken from them in proportions so large as to ... produce ... that monster in civil society, starvation in the midst of abundance.'[21]

This is the essence of Cobbettian political economy, as it was to be that of most political radicals in the 1820s and many in the 1830s. Labour created the wealth of the kingdom. 'Those who labour being the only productive classes in the community, [are] the creators of all wealth, whether in lands, commerce, trade or

navigation.'[22] But that wealth was abstracted from them by those
corruptly wielding political power by means of 'money juggles'
and taxes. The causes of impoverishment, therefore, lay outside
the economic system itself. They were the product of political and
legislative action, whether the Bank Restriction Act of 1797,
which permitted an inflationary expansion of paper money, or the
multiplicity of Acts which imposed or raised taxes 'on your shoes,
salt, beer, malt, hops, tea, sugar, candles, soap, paper, coffee,
spirits, glass of your windows, bricks and tiles, tobacco ... even on
your loaf'.[23] It was political not economic agents who were
central to labour's impoverishment. The exploiters of labour were
fundholders, taxeaters, sinecurists, placemen, borough tyrants,
and it was the place they occupied in a corrupt political system
that gave them the power to impose their exactions on labour.
Thus they were defined with reference to their political not their
economic role.

This perception of exploitation and impoverishment was also
reflected in Cobbett's view of employers. He might have doubts
about the utility of some types of manufacturing and many kinds of
commercial activity and he certainly found repugnant many of the
aesthetic and moral consequences of the conurbations they
produced but, for all that, capitalist entrepreneurs were not seen as
the cause of labour's material distress. Thus both in his *Address to
the Journeymen and Labourers of England*, 1816, and, even more so,
in his *Letter to the Luddites*, 1816, we find Cobbett seeking to dissip-
ate the antagonism which was increasingly expressed towards
employers in a period of falling wages and rising unemployment. In
the former pamphlet he argued, 'on the subject of lowering wages',
that 'you [journeymen and labourers] ought to consider, that your
employers cannot give to you, that which they have not'. Further,
'when journeymen find their wages reduced, they should take time
to reflect on the real cause, before they fly upon their employers,
who are, in many cases, in as great, or greater, distress than themselves'.[24] Similarly, in his *Letter*, while acknowledging that for
labourers to act as they did there must have been

> faults or follies on their [the employers'] side ... I think that we
> shall see, in the sequel, that those circumstances which appear
> to you to have arisen from their avarice, have ... arisen from
> their want of the means, more than from their want of inclina-
> tion, to afford you a competence in exchange for your labour;
> and, I think this, because it is their interest that you should be
> happy and contented.

> It is not machinery; it is not the grinding disposition of your
> employers; it is not improvements in machinery; it is not extor-

tions on the part of bakers and butchers and millers and farmers and corn-dealers, and cheese and butter sellers. It is not to causes of this sort that you ought to attribute your present great and cruel sufferings; but wholly and solely to the great burden of taxes, co-operating with the bubble of paper money.[25]

Again the source of labour's ills is traced not to agents operating within the economic system, but to the action of those located within the political machine.

Inevitably, then, the solution to labour's material distress lay in the political sphere.

Here it is Gentlemen, that you see the real cause of all the calamities that have fallen upon our country, and of all the changes that now threaten it ... You have seen these dangers creep on upon us by slow degrees, but you have seen their pace to be steady. They have never stopped. They keep gathering about us; and he is a very feeble man who expects any remedy, 'till the great cause of the evil be removed that is to say until there shall take place a radical reform of the Commons' House of Parliament.

Only parliamentary reform would lift the 'intolerable weight' which had fallen on the country in general and the journeymen and labourers in particular.[26]

Such ideas dominated the radical press of the immediate post-war period and they were disseminated too in many of the 'unstamped' working-class papers of the 1830s. Yet while they encapsulated the war and post-war experience of a generation of radicals, and while they did, in the immediate post-war period, correctly identify the political roots of some of the major causes of working-class impoverishment, in the decades that followed the war their empirical basis became increasingly weak. If the doctrines of 'Old Corruption' provided a political economy for the working classes, its historical moment was brief.

Even before the end of the war financial and administrative reforms had begun to remove some of the abuses which provided the rhetorical currency of the political economy of political radicalism. As one commentator has put it, 'at least as far back as 1806' government had acted 'to reduce the accuracy of the critique of Old Corruption'.[27] After the war there was a period of substantial retrenchment which saw gross public expenditure fall from £112.9 million in 1815 to £55.5 million a decade later.[28] As early as 1810 a parliamentary committee had concluded that sinecures were an unacceptable means of remunerating past or present public service. Thereafter the numbers were substantially reduced so that by 1833 only 60 remained.[29] Similarly, civil pensions were reduced to a point where their annual cost was negligible, while the number of sinecures fell from around 600 in 1780 to 28 in 1834.[30] 'Economical' and administrative reform was the order of the day both before and after the ending of the war and certainly, by 1830, had played a part in weakening the force of the old corruption critique of existing economic and social relations. Of course, that critique survived into the 1830s but in terms of its purchase on the minds of the working class it was, by then, being challenged by other political economies whose attractiveness lay in their explanation of impoverishment in economic rather than political terms and their formulation of a theory of exploitation more consistent with the experience of those who lived and worked in the period of nascent industrial capitalism.

In this context one final point can be made about Cobbettian political economy. Though, when finally elected to parliament, he sat for Preston, a northern, industrial constituency, Cobbett's writing was permeated throughout by an essential incomprehension of, and antipathy to, the increasing industrialisation of the economy and commercialisation of economic life. This anti-commercialism and anti-urbanism were expressed with particular vehemence in a series of letters published in the *Political Register*, during 1807 and 1808, under the expressive title of *Perish Commerce!* Here he was to argue that 'commerce had been the cause of our national decline'. It had 'erected a sort of undergovernment' which ensured that when government policy was formulated 'upon almost every occasion, the question has been, not what is just but what is expedient, the expediency turning solely upon the interests of commerce'. Commercial considerations had come to dominate decision-making and national honour offered up by way of sacrifice. Commerce had also 'assembled ... men together in large bodies, which never fails to enervate the mind and to produce an effeminacy of taste and manners, not to mention the numerous vices, which now disgrace this country'. It was at the root of the rapid urbanisation which had created, for example, the 'Great Wen' of London, where 'half a million of persons ... are constantly employed in nothing but the annihilation of the produce of land'.[31]

Reversing the process of commercialisation and urbanisation would, in contrast, 'give new life to useful industry and would cause many to labour who now live in idleness ... it must tend to elevate agriculture and every species of useful manufacture; and ... it would exalt human nature itself, by banishing from amongst us a part, at least, of that effeminacy, and of those corruptions which now issue from the metropolis and other trading places, as from another Pandora's box to vitiate the country'. Similarly, a decline in manufacturing in favour of agriculture should be welcomed as those employed in the latter would be 'more hale and stout sort of men than the latter ... less exposed to those vices which the congregating of men never fails to produce'. This would render 'the nation better and more powerful than it now is'.[32]

Cobbett's antipathy to commerce and all that he saw as following from it, in terms of the growth of towns and the excessive expansion of manufacturing activity, was expressed with particular vehemence in *Perish Commerce!* But one can dip into Cobbett's substantial literary output almost at random and come up with similar sentiments. They run like a leitmotif through, for example, the most popular of all his works – *Rural Rides* – and, to the extent that they formed such an integral part of his economic and social thought, we have here a political economy which would, increasingly, have jarred on the sensibilities of those whose interests it purported to articulate. To be told that 'agriculture is the only source of wealth', that manufacturing activity was, in many respects, parasitic, that cities effeminised and induced intellectual torpor in their inhabitants, that it was agriculture that produced a hale, hearty, virtuous and virile population was to articulate a political economy which missed the mark of a growing urban working class. In this regard it is both poignant and significant that when Cobbett died, on 13 June 1835, he did so talking about his crops.

CHAPTER 3

Some Aspects of a Changing Economy, 1815–50

Spencean political economy clearly reflected the extent to which, in the eighteenth century, political and economic authority were derived from landed property. Cobbett's political economy of Old Corruption was also predicated upon such a view of things, while recognising too some of the new sources of power which emerged out of the exigencies of war. Given the dominant position of agriculture in the late eighteenth- and early nineteenth-century British economy, such conceptions of the bases of economic domination and thence the causes of labour's impoverishment were, and remained for some time, well founded. Yet, for all that, the period 1800–50 did see a fundamental shift in the locus of economic power – something that was to have a profound bearing on the evolution of socialist and anti-capitalist political economy in Britain in those years.

However, before considering that evolution in detail, it is necessary to understand some aspects of the nature and complexity of the shift and its consequences. To begin with it is important to note that most economic historians now emphasise the slowness and incremental nature of change, the persistence of earlier forms of economic organisation and, more generally, continuity rather than revolution as the characteristics of economic development in this period. Thus, for example, artisan and small workshop production, together with cottage industry, remained of considerable importance well into the nineteenth century. It is interesting to note that the epithet elicited by Britain's mid-century dominance of the global economy was 'workshop [not factory] of the world'. Yet this stress on continuity, and the associated tendency to call into question the concept of an industrial *revolution*, should not obscure the profound economic and social changes that did occur.

If, as late as 1850, artisans and small workshops were a more characteristic feature of the British economy than steam-driven machinery and factory production, it was none the less true that, in many instances, the status of the artisan, the organisation of the workshop, the nature of the production that characterised it and the technology that was deployed within its confines, had changed fundamentally over the previous half-century. As one commentator has put it: 'what was painful to workshop owners and their workforce in this period was not so much the problem of eclipse and absorption by the factory, but rather their transformation'.[1] As regards this transformation, the position of the artisan, in many trades, was being increasingly undermined by growing competitive pressures.[2] These took a number of forms and had a variety of consequences.

First, there was the competition resulting from the growth of 'dishonourable' masters or middlemen who used supplies of cheap, unskilled labour and refused to adhere to the prices and wages viewed as customary in a trade. This was due in part to the increasing importance of subcontracting in many trades in the early nineteenth century which could, on the one hand, force some to become, in effect, small capitalist masters or middlemen, breaking with the rules and customs that had previously governed their behaviour as artisans. On the other, those who did not assume that role could find themselves the victims rather than the perpetrators of 'sweating'. To the extent that this occurred, their status clearly approximated more closely to that of wage labour. Either way the independence and autonomy of the artisan was being eroded, and with it the power and/or the inclination to adhere, or ensure adherence, to customary practices, prices and rewards. Where this happened, the relationship in the workshop increasingly became that between capitalist employer and hired labourer, not master craftsman and apprentice. As one commentator has written: 'capitalism in the early nineteenth century made progress less by machines and factories than by the increasing control of the small workshop by capitalist middlemen, through their power over credit, supply and distribution'. Using such power it was they who often altered 'the tempo and quality of workshop life'.[3] Such developments were reflected in the critical analysis of anti-capitalist and socialist political economists of the period and also, as we shall see in the next chapter, in the work of those who sought to formulate a moral political economy.

Second, changed methods of production which involved a degree of de-skilling opened up the possibility of competition from an unskilled, 'sweated' workforce – one that increasingly included child and female labour. This was a labour force that, for demographic reasons, was also growing rapidly, thereby further intensifying competitive pressures.

Third, legislative changes, such as the repeal of the apprenticeship (1813) and wage regulation clauses (1814) of the Statute of Artificers, 1563, dismantled the general regulatory legal framework within which many trades had been conducted.[4] Legislation specific to particular trades, such as the Spitalfields Acts (1773) governing wages and prices in the silk-weaving trade, remained on the statute books, but even here regulation did not long survive the ending of the Napoleonic Wars, the Spitalfields Acts being repealed in 1824. Also, as regards the regulative activity of the state, the Combination Acts of 1799 and 1800 not only involved the state adopting a repressive stance with respect to trade unions, but also its withdrawal from 'an older "regulative" role in the determination of the price of labour'.[5] Thus, while suppressing those organisations that had previously played a major role in the defence of traditional rates and rights, the Acts failed to furnish any compensatory legislative protection.

This progressive, competitive erosion of the independence of significant elements of the artisanate, the relative diminution in the importance of independent producers, the change in the nature and organisation of workshop production, the growth in subcontracting and the concomitant increase in 'sweating', the expansion of the putting out system, often as a consequence of mechanisation – all contributed to the increasing proletarianisation of labour which, as one commentator has phrased it, 'was the dominant process of the age'.[6] As we shall see, the anti-capitalist and socialist political economy that emerged in the first half of the nineteenth century, both as regards its critical analysis and in terms of the economic and social arrangements that it proposed, reflected in many respects the experience and the concerns of an artisanate increasingly threatened with a debasement of its status to that of hired hands.

Further, with respect to the growth of an industrial proletariat, while the factory was clearly not the characteristic form of manufacturing activity in the first half of the nineteenth century, it was none the less an increasingly significant type of industrial organisation, most obviously in the textile and iron industries. There was, more generally, a growth in the scale of manufacturing enterprises. Thus while in the late eighteenth century only one third of cotton spinning mills employed more than 50 workers, by 1830 the average size of a cotton factory workforce was 175.5; the figure for silk being 93.3, though for woollen mills it was still only 44.6.[7] As regards the linen industry, while the first mills were not built in Scotland until the 1780s, in Dundee alone, 'by 1822, there were seventeen steam-powered flax mills, employing 2,000 people, plus another 32 mills in the neighbourhood'. In Birmingham, the first half of the nineteenth century saw the growth of large manufactories in the metallurgical sector and, increasingly, the dominance of large capital-intensive firms.[8] Of course, the pace of these developments should not be overstated, nor should the continuing importance of small-scale production and the role of the artisan in the early nineteenth-century British economy be underplayed. That said, these developments too contributed to the process of proletarianisation, diminishing the possibility of economic independence for the labourer, widening the gulf between the buyers and sellers of labour and increasing the power wielded by the former relative to the latter. Again, such developments were to be discussed and theorised in the anti-capitalist and socialist political economy of the period to 1850.

Nor was this process of proletarianisation confined to the manufacturing sector, as Chapter 1 has made clear. In agriculture also the extinction of common rights, consequent upon enclosure, the decline in the practice of agricultural labourers 'living in' with their employer and other developments made for an increasing dependence of agricultural labour on wages. As one writer has put it with respect to these developments in the Midlands:

> the domestic economy of the whole village was radically altered. No longer could the peasant derive the necessaries of life from the materials, the soil, and the resources of his own countryside and his own strong arms. The self-supporting peasant was transformed into a spender of money, for all the things he needed were now in the shops. Money, which in the sixteenth century had played merely a marginal though a necessary, part, now became the only thing necessary for the maintenance of life.[9]

Thus the late eighteenth and early nineteenth centuries witnessed the growth of a rural proletariat, a development that found expression in the agitation over *wages* which occurred in the south and east of England in the period 1793–1805 and, more dramatically and bloodily, in East Anglia in the immediate post-Napoleonic Wars period.[10]

As the nineteenth century progressed, therefore, labour became increasingly a marketable commodity, denied easy access to the means of production and dependent on the successful sale of its services for its means of subsistence and so upon those with the power to make that purchase. In addition, the buyers of labour – industrial, merchant and agrarian capitalists – were becoming relatively more powerful, exerting their control over growing numbers of propertyless labourers and becoming increasingly distant from those whom they employed. However gradual the process, however uneven the development as between sectors and geographical areas, the proletarianisation of labour was something on which contemporary commentators remarked and on which those critical of existing economic and social arrangements inevitably focused.

The buying and selling of labour aside, it should be noted too that while the contractual relationship between the buyers and sellers of food had also previously been mediated, in some measure, by moral and customary presuppositions and by legislation which gave judicial effect to these, by the late eighteenth and early nineteenth centuries that was also ceasing to be the case. In the eighteenth century, as E.P. Thompson and others have shown, 'the English crowd' frequently acted by way of riot and other forms of direct action to prevent the price of corn and bread from deviating significantly from what custom dictated was a just price. Further, legislation against forestalling and regrating, and institutions such as the Assize of Bread in London, provided legislative buttresses for a moral economy which, if policed by popular sentiment, could also often count on the support of the local magistracy. However, the legislation against forestalling was repealed in 1772, the Assize of Bread was abolished in 1815, while the effectiveness of 'the moral economy of the English crowd' inevitably diminished with proletarianisation in general and the growth of an industrial proletariat in particular; the latter shifting the concern surrounding the means of subsistence from the price of food to the level of wages. Again, as with the other developments noticed, the increasing importance of unmediated market relations rather than economic relations mediated by custom or popular morality was something that was to leave its mark on the anti-capitalist and socialist political economy which emerged in the first half of the nineteenth century; not least in the concern of some to set the notion of a just price on a basis that was both theoretically coherent and a guide to practical action. Inevitably, also, the growing strength of amoral market forces provoked those who sought the reconstitution of a moral economy.

It should be noted too that as untrammelled market forces grew in potency, money necessarily acquired a growing significance for the working class. The growth of a labour force divorced from the land and, in addition, the general process of proletarianisation, meant that labour was increasingly dependent on the monetisation of its services to survive. The custom of payment in kind remained, in some trades for most of the rest of the century, but it diminished in significance, as too did remuneration in the form of perquisites – the 'waste' from productive activity claimed by those such as shipwrights, tailors, porters and weavers.[11] Money – specifically, the money wage – was, more and more, what provided the means of life and determined its quality. Further, its significance for the working class was growing rapidly just at a time when its value became increasingly unstable. It has already been noted that between 1788/92 and 1809/15 the value of money depreciated by between 65 per cent and 85 per cent; while in the post-war period there was an equally dramatic appreciation with the general price index falling from 202 in 1814 to 116 in 1822.[12] Rapid price inflation, followed by an equally sharp deflation, imparted an unparalleled volatility to economic relations which were increasingly mediated by money. The sentiments of Keynes expressed with reference to comparable price fluctuations after the Great War are apposite here. They 'redistributed Fortune's favours so as to frustrate design and disappoint expectation' and in so doing, of course, raised fundamental questions about the nature and worth of money in the minds of anti-capitalist and socialist writers.

It was also the case that in the context of such a fluid, disordered, unstable and periodically depressed macroeconomic backdrop, the changes in the organisation of industry, noted above, and the developments set in motion by technical innovation, almost inevitably made for widening social divisions and heightened social antagonism. Within the workshop, tensions were exacerbated as the paternalist master craftsman under competitive pressures intermittently intensified by depession and the technological dispacement of labour, was transmuted into a 'sweating' employer, while the skilled apprentice was downgraded into an employee whose product or services were bought cheap and sold dear. As Behagg has written:

> a case could be made for the severity of the struggle between employer and employee being far greater in the workshop than in the large factory ... The [market] imperatives to reorganise work and thus enhance employer control could ... be greater in the smaller unit of production where profits were slimmer and market viability more tenuous.[13]

Similarly, where mechanisation and other developments produced an expansion of outworking in a situation of labour surplus and falling prices, the business of buying and selling necessarily became a source, and the market a locus, of rising social tension and conflict.

Further, while, as has been said, the progress of the factory system may indeed have been slow and other types of industrial organisation relatively more important throughout the early nineteenth century, the increasing size of industrial enterprises nevertheless made not only for a greater social and material gulf between the buyers and sellers of labour but also exacerbated an existing and fundamental imbalance of bargaining power in favour of the increasingly capitalised employer. Thus even Joyce, who has stressed the extent to which their interdependence was recognised and articulated by both capitalists and labourers and who has emphasised too the degree to which they negotiated differences on a 'terrain of compromise', has none the less made clear that in the early nineteenth century this relationship would not have been experienced as a 'relationship of equals: the effect of dependence and economic insecurity led to accommodations with capital based on coercion and necessity'.[14]

Whether the process of proletarianisation, the growing imbalance of bargaining power and the widening socio-economic gulf between increasingly capitalised employers and capital-less wage labourers laid the basis for the emergence of a distinctive working-class consciousness is, of course, a moot point and one beyond the scope of the present study. It will, however, be argued in later chapters that these developments did leave their imprint on the anti-capitalist and socialist political economy of the period and precipitated the formulation of an economic language of class and class antagonism. Before discussing the work of such writers, though, it is important to consider those who used a different economic discourse and formulated a different kind of political economy for the working class. Such a consideration is important because these writers articulated the experience and expressed the views of significant groups of early nineteenth-century labourers. In addition, theirs was a language that clearly had deep roots in popular consciousness and was one indeed that often surfaced, even if deployed with different theoretical intent, in the work of many of those anti-capitalist and socialist writers who will be considered in later chapters. These were the moral economists who, particularly in the 1820s and 1830s, formulated a political economy that had a specific resonance for that part of the working class whose livelihood and status, previously buttressed by custom, tradition and popular notions of economic justice, was now acutely threatened with destruction by the amoral forces which competitive capitalism had unleashed.

CHAPTER 4

A Moral Political Economy

Economically and politically the immediate post-Napoleonic Wars period proved turbulent. On the economic side this manifested itself most obviously in the economic depression of 1816–19, a period characterised by mass unemployment, a marked fall in prices and widespread bankruptcies, as a reduction in government expenditure, the structural adjustments necessary in the transition from war to peace and a tightening of monetary policy impacted adversely on the general level of productive activity. In such circumstances, with overstocked labour and commodity markets, competition intensified and pressure mounted on customary work practices, workloads, prices and remuneration. At the same time, as was noted in the previous chapter, what remained of the legislative buttresses of a moral economy, where productive activity occurred within a framework grounded on customary notions of fairness and justice, had already, in large part, been dismantled even before the cessation of hostilities. This assault continued in the post-war period, with such measures as the repeal of the Spitalfields Acts, 1824. Further, the repeal of the Combination Acts in the same year, while making legitimate a narrow range of trade union activities, none the less confirmed the abandonment of any state regulation of the labour market.

It has been argued that legislation such as the wage fixing and apprenticeship clauses of the Statute of Artificers[1] had, to a large extent, fallen into desuetude by the early nineteenth century and that, therefore, what occurred simply solemnised, legislatively, the moral economy's effective demise. Yet this argument is problematic. As regards the apprenticeship clauses, repeal came at a time when the influx of unskilled or semi-skilled labour into many trades[2] had renewed interest in statutory support for the apprenticeship system. Also, the prolonged dispute over the Spitalfields Acts illustrates the degree of support from some sections of the workforce, from many masters and, on occasion, from within Parliament, for legislative sanction of customary and moral economic norms.[3] As regards parliamentary support, for example, a Select Committee on Silk Weavers' Petitions, 1818, stated that it was of the opinion that it is absolutely necessary, for the protection of the weavers in the silk trade and the ribbon trade in particular, and to enable them to support themselves and families ... that some legislative interference should take place; and your Committee think, that a remedy would be found in the extension of the provision of the Spitalfields ... Acts, or at least a trial of that extension for a period of a few years, by way of experiment.[4]

So, while economic circumstances and *laissez-faire* principles might combine to devastating legislative and ideological effect, the onslaught did not go unresisted, and indeed the economic philosophy of a moral economy received, in the 1820s and 1830s, some of its fullest and most eloquent expressions, just as that economy was receiving its statutory *coup de grâce*.

These came from the protagonists of groups such as the framework knitters and the silk, wool and cotton handloom weavers, who penned tracts, petitions and pamphlets defending workers on whom the impact of market forces had broken with particular violence in this period. Consciously engaging with the classical economists and their popularisers they evoked the spirit and deployed the discourse of a moral political economy and proposed, like Gravenor Henson, leader of the framework knitters, the reconstitution of an economy characterised by 'certainty and stability', where 'the operatives [were] ... not being suddenly overwhelmed and deprived of the two inestimable blessings, moderate wages and regular employment'.[5]

That they knew the nature of the ideological beast with which they wrestled is clear from their writings. 'It is frequently asserted', wrote Robert Hall in 1820, 'that the rate of wages, like every other article, should be left to find its own level and that all attempts at artificial regulations, either by voluntary association or legal enactment, are repugnant to the true principles of political economy'. Indeed it was. Giving evidence to the select committee mentioned above, one owner of a silk manufactory stated he was 'of the opinion ... that every regulation that interferes with a manufacture is useless, hurtful, dangerous. It unsettles the workmen, repels the artist, blunts industry, disgusts the consumer, discredits the seller and ruins the enterprise'. Other manufacturers were to express similar sentiments.[6] And it was those who adhered to such views, those 'who advocat[ed] the doctrine of labour being left to find its own level, of the poor being left to the mercy of their employers without any protection', who were unreservedly damned by the moral economists as 'either very ignorant or very great enemies to the working classes';[7] their *laissez-faire* stance being rebutted along four complementary lines.

To begin with, argued Hall and others: 'it is evident that the vaunted maxim of leaving every kind of production and labour to find its own level is not adhered to ... it has always been violated in this country from the remotest times'.[8] The fact was that types of property other than labour had secured and continued to secure legislative protection. Most obviously (and most recently) the passage of the Corn Laws had highlighted the preparedness of the legislature to interfere with market forces in order to protect the landowning interests. *A Petition from the Journeymen Broad Silk Weavers*, 1828, made just this point when it pronounced it fundamentally unjust 'that the incomes and property of all other classes should be protected, whilst the Artisans and Labourers alone are left a prey to be plundered by needy, rapacious, and unprincipled Employers'.[9] In the absence of a market where the recompense of productive factors was freely determined, the advantages to be secured from the unconstrained operation of natural economic laws assumed a purely theoretical significance. Those who preached these advantages were either misguided or, more likely, self-interested. Either way intervention was necessary to redress this legislative imbalance.

Second, writers remarked on the collusive instincts of employers and their tendency to combine to lower the wages of labour. Labourers confronted not employers competing for their services but those whose collusion often gave them monopsonistic powers. Here Adam Smith proved of considerable service, and writers quoted that passage in the *Wealth of Nations* where Smith described 'masters as [being] always and every where in a sort of tacit, but constant and uniform combination, not to raise the wages of labour above their actual rate', and where he also remarked that the reason 'we seldom, indeed, hear of this combination, is because it is the usual, and one may say, the natural state of things'. Smith's further observation that 'we have no acts of parliament against combining to lower the price of work; but many against combining to raise it' was similarly applauded.[10] Even the *Wealth of Nations* made clear, therefore, that those whose political economy was predicated on the existence of free markets were working with a purely imaginative construct and one used to obfuscate the reality of collusive exploitation.

Third, many commentators stressed the distinctive nature of labour as a commodity and the implications this had for its position in the market. Thus 'the situation of the labourer [was] widely different' from that of the buyers and sellers of other goods and services, for 'he has no other article to dispose of besides his personal industry and skill'. The consequent imperative to sell meant that the labourer could not 'without being reduced to immediate distress withhold them [his services] from the market'.[11] So the putative scope for haggling was, in practice, severely circumscribed, with bargaining power decidedly skewed in favour of the purchaser of labour power. Further, not only was 'labour ... the only commodity the artisan has to part with', it was also 'of such a nature it will not permit him to adjust the supply to the demand'.[12] In this context mechanisation and the resultant displacement of labour were seen as compounding the imbalance between the former and the latter. Labour's vulnerability to exploitation was therefore an integral feature of any 'system of anarchical free trade'.[13]

Finally, it was argued that this skewed distribution of market power was exacerbated by what the ownership of capital conferred. While in some sense both labourers and capitalists were price-takers, the latter could take judiciously and selectively, free from the imperative of want which drove labour to accept only what was immediately on offer. 'Capital', which was clearly identified as 'the fruits of the industry of the working classes', 'enable[d] persons who are in trade to withhold their goods from the market, when they cannot obtain a remunerating price, and it enable[d] them to take advantage of the market when there is a brisk demand for goods to obtain a higher price for them'.[14] The owners of capital possessed exactly that power denied to the labourer: the power to act with that rationality and foresight which the popularisers of classical political economy saw as the prerogative of all market participants.[15]

The primary objective of these moral economists was that economic activity should be conducted by reference to different principles and should pursue different objectives from those which, increasingly, were coming to govern it. First, and most importantly, it should be driven by ethical imperatives rather than egotistic impulses. The language used to constitute this new moral world was redolent of this and represented a discursive terrain far removed from that of classical political economy. Thus as regards the price of labour: this should be determined not as the by-product of the predatory pursuit of profit, but with reference to the principles of equity, justice, need and desert. '*Reason and justice* require that the workman's wages should enable him to provide decent clothing and suitable education for his children'; they should be sufficient 'to procure the necessaries of life for himself and his family'. This was what constituted a '*just and natural remuneration*', 'a *just price*', 'a *fair and equitable price*', 'a *living price*' for labour.[16] 'Wages' should be 'equal to the *merit* of *honest* productive labour', yielding '*merited* comfort' to the labourer and his family.[17] Wage rates should not emerge as the unconsidered outcome of the operation of impersonal market forces. Still less should they be determined by the *force majeure* of employers acting individually or in concert. Rather they should be consciously determined by reference to custom, human and occupational needs, labour effort and a communal sense of fairness. In turn the 'master' should be 'enabled to derive a *fair* profit' with 'no ruinous home competition' allowed to 'suddenly arise to overwhelm him'.[18] Nor, for that matter, should he have to suffer the exploitation of their bargaining power by workers 'when the trade happens to be in a flourishing state'.[19] This was the basis and this the discourse of a morally constituted economy; an economy where any exercise of coercive economic power was to be curbed and which proceeded, therefore, on the basis of fair dealing between masters and men.

But who should be the architects of this moral economy and how should it be constructed? A variety of answers emerged. Some argued that as 'the great end' of 'Government ... is to prevent one man from taking undue advantage, by withholding or abstracting from him his fair share of the fruits of his industry, and which share is the value of his products', it was manifestly the responsibility of the state to ensure that justice and equity determined distributive outcomes.[20] As with the Spitalfields Acts this might involve the judiciary enforcing a set of 'standard prices' for particular kinds of work. So, 'in case of difference as to what is a reasonable price to be paid for any work, there is a competent tribunal to which both parties can apply, and which, after hearing evidence' would 'decide fairly between them', 'secur[ing] to the journeymen a fair compensation only for their labour, and prevent[ing] their demanding an extravagant price in brisk trade'.[21] Also, in terms of government intervention, the idea of a legally enforced minimum wage was strongly advocated. Thus defending the interests of the framework knitters Robert Hall wrote in 1820: 'if every other expedient should fail, we see no reason why its [the legislature's] aid should not be exerted in favour of the Leicestershire framework knitters as well as of the Spitalfields weavers, who were a few years ago effectually relieved by the establishment of a minimum'.[22] Such minima might also be fixed and policed, as they had been in the past, by local magistrates. As one writer phrased it, 'to fix a minimum is absolutely necessary; justice requires it because it is the proper business of the Magistrate to prevent one part of society from oppressing another'.[23] In this context too emphasis was also put on intervention to counterbalance the legislative protection already enjoyed by other interests in society. One specific proposal came from John Maxwell who, in a pamphlet entitled *Machinery versus Manual Labour*, 1834, argued that machinery should be taxed to put it on a competitive par with labour, an essential component of whose subsistence had already been taxed by the introduction of the Corn Laws. On similar grounds an anonymous *Petition* argued that unless the legislature acted 'immediately [to] ... abolish all existing monopolies, admit an unrestrained importation of Corn, and all other articles of subsistence and comfort, and to reduce the salaries and pay of all Placemen and Pensioners' and so 'cause a reduction of Taxation equivalent to the reduction in the rate of Wages', it should, in fairness, intervene to regulate the level of wages and prices.[24] Only if it removed legislative protection from *all* would it have acted even-handedly and in a way consistent with the *laissez-faire* principles it sometimes professed. Only then would it have fulfilled its responsibility to protect all interests equally. Of course, the expectation was that it would not do so. Vested interests would prevent it acting in such a manner and so it should therefore, in conscience and consistency, give to labour the protection which it bestowed on others.

However, the institutional framework necessary to achieve the moral economists' objectives was also conceived of in self-regulatory terms. One writer, again drawing on past precedent, suggested 'establishing Boards of Trade to fix for assigned periods what shall be the minimum wages to be paid for standard fabrics'. Others looked to the 'sanction of the legislature [for] any MUTUAL COMPACT OF MASTERS AND MEN ... to secure such wages as the manufacturer can pay, without impairing his sales, diminishing the demand of purchasers, or exposing himself to the competition of some rash adventurer'. Here the aim was legislative reinforcement of a morally rooted voluntary compact between employers and employees which ensured 'fair and equitable' rewards for all.[25]

Finally, there were suggestions as to how labourers themselves might act to place or to re-establish their trades on an 'honourable' basis. Thus the idea of a fund that could be used to give work or support to unemployed framework knitters was mooted. This would improve the competitive position of those who remained and create the possibility of a rise in wages to 'fair and equitable' levels. It would 'afford a subsistence ... to that portion of the labouring class who are destitute of employment, that they may not be compelled to offer their labour for next to nothing, and thus reduce the general rate of wages'.[26] Similarly, there was the idea of a fund to purchase stocking frames, which would then be let out on condition that their users 'should not work under the regular price obtained by the trade'.[27] Here writers were in some measure countenancing the market determination of rewards, though in a context where the imbalance in bargaining power had been redressed or, at least, considerably reduced. Yet whatever the expedients suggested the overarching goal was the same.

Economic life was to be made to dance to a different tune and economic activity proceed on an altered basis and with different objectives from those that characterised contemporary industrial capitalism. Economic and social harmony was to be engendered not by the operations of an invisible hand but by the creation of a legislative and institutional framework which ensured that economic activity proceeded according to certain collectively agreed moral and customary norms.

Such ideas left their mark on the silk weavers, the framework knitters, the wool and cotton handloom weavers and other groups of workers as they struggled vainly in the early nineteenth century for what they deemed a reasonable subsistence. Echoes of them can also be found, as we shall see, in the socialist political economy of the period. They were to surface again in new model union demands for a 'fair day's pay for a fair day's work' and, as recent research has shown, they were to re-emerge to prove influential in labour bargaining in the mid-century Lancashire cotton textile industry.[28] Moral notions also infused the political economy of Christian socialists such as F.D. Maurice, E.V. Neale and J.M. Ludlow in the 1850s and 1860s and, in the 1890s, that of Robert Blatchford and others who demanded a *'living wage'* for labour.

But the work of the moral economists was painfully vulnerable to rebuttal by the classical economists and their popularisers whose arguments proceeded on the basis of 'is' not 'ought' and who claimed, as the formulators and interpreters of *natural* economic laws, to speak with the authority of science not the aspiration of ethics. Thus for writers such as Harriet Martineau, Charles Knight, James Mill and others, the prices that emerged from the impersonal play of market forces reflected the *natural* value of commodities and ensured a recompense to all factors of production and their owners commensurate with their contribution to productive activity. Equity was not guaranteed by a legislative recognition and balancing of the competing economic claims of different social groups but by a mechanism that was immune from the malign manipulation of particular vested interests. Economic justice was a consequence not of the conscious deliberations of magistrates, boards of trade, the collusion of masters and men or the actions of legislatures, but was bestowed by an invisible hand, which transmuted the self-interested pursuit of gain into social benefits.

To such a view of the economic world the moral economists had, as we have seen, a set of ripostes but it had little purchase on the arguments of those whose analysis and prescriptions proceeded on an economic rather than a moral terrain.[29] In addition, the constituency whose position they aimed, primarily, to defend was shrinking as market forces confirmed their worst fears and effected the economic destruction of weavers and knitters as independent producers. Moreover, economic policy after 1815 clearly evolved in a manner that showed that those wielding political power had succumbed, in greater or lesser measure, to the notion that the liberalisation not the moralisation of trade was in the best interests of the community. The dismantling of the legislative buttresses of a moral economy has already been mentioned and there was precious little indication, in the early nineteenth century, that they would be replaced. The work of the moral economists was, in many ways, a swansong. It traced the lineaments and sang the praises of an economic world soon to be irrevocably lost. For all its moral fire and ethical eloquence this was a political economy whose time had largely passed. For a more effective rebuttal of classical ideas and for a political economy which did address the complex and multifarious economic evils of nascent industrial capitalism the working class were, increasingly, to look elsewhere.

CHAPTER 5

Thomas Hodgskin: Anti-capitalist

Thomas Hodgskin was born in Chatham on 12 December 1787. A naval cadet at the age of twelve, he remained in the navy until 1812 when he was court-martialled and retired on half pay for accusing his captain of victimisation. This experience and his time in the navy left him with an antipathy to the arbitrary and coercive exercise of power, sentiments which were to find expression in *An Essay on Naval Discipline*, 1813, and which ran as a unifying theme throughout the totality of his work. After two years in Edinburgh (1813–15) pursuing courses at the university, he returned to London, became acquainted with Francis Place and, through him, was brought into contact with Jeremy Bentham, James Mill and the intellectual currents of utilitarianism and classical political economy.[1]

The first book in which he touched directly on economic questions was his *Travels in the North of Germany*, 1820, which came out of a three-year tour in post-Napoleonic Wars Europe. Again Hodgskin focused on, among other things, the malign exercise of authority, this time by governments which he condemned for the tolls which they had imposed on road and river transport and for their granting of trade and other monopolies. Thus in this context, and in a manner strongly reminiscent of Adam Smith, he argued that 'whatever the state regulates becomes bloated and withered, and whatever it leaves to the unfettered sense of the people prospers'. Comparing the position of the north German states adversely with that of Britain, he also wrote that in the latter 'individual interest sharpened by competition animates and directs the whole'.[2] However, if Smith's influence may have been important in shaping such views,[3] so also was Hodgskin's deistic conception of the world as naturally harmonious and governed by laws promulgated by a beneficent deity. Such a perception of things led Hodgskin to see human laws in general, and those that affected economic activity in particular, as at best superfluous and at worst productive of injustice and impoverishment. This was a view for which he was, in large measure, indebted to the theologian William Paley's *Principles of Moral and Political Philosophy*, 1785, though it should be said that it was also a common conception of the world by the late eighteenth century.[4] It was this view of a naturally harmonious material and moral order which informed the totality of his writing on political economy and dictated an adherence to a *laissez-faire* in many respects more consistent and extreme than any articulated by the classical political economists.

In the 1820s Hodgskin helped to establish and jointly edited a weekly journal, the *Mechanics' Magazine* (1823–24) which, together with the part he played in establishing the London Mechanics' Institute, brought him into contact with the artisans and mechanics who occupied such an important place in the economy of the capital. For the most part the paper was concerned with popular science, but Hodgskin did contribute articles in which he sought to dissuade Spitalfields silk weavers from agitating against the repeal of those Acts (1773) that permitted the magistrates of the City of London to fix the wages of labour in their industry. Again, anti-statist and anti-authority arguments were prominent.

Also, in 1824, he became involved in a bitter struggle over the management of the London Mechanics' Institute. This revolved around the issue of executive authority and whether it should reside in the hands of the 'mechanics' or in those of the Institute's middle-class benefactors and subscribers. This brought Hodgskin into conflict with those such as Francis Place and James Mill who had previously proved influential and who had helped to advance Hodgskin's career. This conflict was to acquire a more overtly ideological character in three works which were to establish his reputation as one of the most important anti-capitalist political economists of the nineteenth century – *Labour Defended against the Claims of Capital*, 1825, *Popular Political Economy, Four Lectures Delivered at the London Mechanics' Institute*, 1827 and *The Natural and Artificial Rights of Property Contrasted*, 1832.

What strikes one immediately about these works is the extent to which they embraced the concepts and analytical devices of classical political economy,[5] something which immediately distinguished the analysis, critical thrust and language of Hodgskin's attack on existing economic arrangements both from that of the moral economists and also contemporary radicals such as William Cobbett. With Hodgskin, we have a qualitatively different kind of assault on contemporary economic evils. When Cobbett, for example, used the language of 'Old Corruption', he was deploying an essentially political rhetoric. Economic evils and, in particular, the poverty of the many were, for him, the product of a corrupt system of government which used taxation and the financial system to underwrite the patronage necessary for its survival. Sinecurists, placemen, boroughmongers and a venal aristocracy were the cause of poverty and the remedy was a parliamentary reform which would destroy the roots of their political power. The exploitation of the working class had, therefore, a political basis and so cried out for a political remedy. Hodgskin, in contrast, sought the causes of the impoverishment of the working class in the economic sphere. In analysing those causes he adopted the tripartite, class division of society favoured by most of the classical political economists in their theories of distribution. Thus, for example, Ricardo in his *Principles of Political Economy and Taxation*, 1817, saw 'the principal problem in Political Economy' as that of determining the laws which regulated the distribution of the national product among the 'three classes of the community ... the proprietors of the land, the owner of the stock or capital ... and the labourers'.[6]

Considering, then, the question of distribution in relation to the economic role of these classes, Hodgskin argued from the premise that labour alone was productive of value and that neither the landowner nor the capitalist furnished labour for the productive process, to the conclusion that 'the whole produce of labour ought to belong to the labourer'.[7] In fact, what labour furnished by its efforts, under existing economic arrangements, largely accrued to the landowning and capitalist class, with labour receiving only what was necessary for its subsistence and reproduction. So while Malthus might explain poverty by reference to surplus population and Ricardo in terms of the limits set to production by available cultivable land, for Hodgskin the root cause was a distribution of wealth in which landowners and capitalists shared but to the creation of which they failed to contribute.

However, it is important to note here that while Hodgskin was at pains to emphasise that the rental income which landowners received was unwarranted and represented an appropriation of what rightfully belonged to labour, the exaction of rent was not, as he saw it, the primary cause of working-class impoverishment. 'To produce this surplus would not break the back, and to give it up would not break the heart of the labourer. The landlord's share, therefore, does not keep the labourer poor'. As Hodgskin saw it, following Ricardo: 'the landowners do only receive, and ever have only received the surplus produce of the more fertile soils'.[8] The crucial exactions were those imposed by capital for 'all the rest of the whole produce of labour in this and in every country goes to the capitalist under the name of profit for the use of his capital'. 'CAPITAL and CAPITALISTS ... have long since reduced the ancient tyrant of the soil to comparative insignificance, while they have inherited his power over all the labouring classes. It is, therefore, now time that the reproaches so long cast on the feudal aristocracy should be heaped on capital and capitalists.'[9]

In *Labour Defended* Hodgskin highlighted the new source of exploitative power which was emerging. In marked contrast to

Thomas Spence it was, for Hodgskin, no longer the ownership of land that was decisive as regards the indigence of labour but rather the ownership of capital. This also distinguished him clearly from classical writers who, like Ricardo, saw the expanding share of rent in the national income as the major obstacle in the way of economic progress. For Hodgskin it was not the income resulting from the landowner's monopoly of a finite resource which was the problem. Rather it was 'capital which ... engross[ing] the whole produce of a country, except the bare subsistence of the labourer, and the surplus produce of fertile land', was the cause of the economic ills which labour experienced.[10] For Hodgskin, this engrossing was accomplished by the power that the capitalist possessed to effect a deviation of 'social price' from 'natural value'; the latter being determined by 'the whole quantity of labour nature requires from man that he may produce any commodity' and the former, crucially, by the addition of profits (though also rents) to natural (labour) values.[11] Thus it was in the sphere of exchange that labour was exploited, being forced to sell its labour too cheap for commodities which, because their price embodied profit and rent, were (relative to their natural value) too dear.

Contemporary writers frequently justified the income of the capitalist by reference to the value which fixed and circulating capital contributed to the production process and as a reward for the saving (abstinence) involved in making that capital available to the workforce. But Hodgskin would have none of this. Circulating capital, the value of the subsistence advanced to labour and the value of raw materials utilised in production, did not constitute, as classical economists and their popularisers would have it, a pre-existing stock of goods frugally accumulated by the capitalist and for which he deserved recompense. Rather what was termed circulating capital was, in effect, 'co-existing labour'. 'No species of labour depends on any previously prepared stock', wrote Hodgskin, 'for in fact no such stock exists; but every species of labour does constantly, and at all times, depend for his supplies on the co-existing labour of some other labourers'.[12] The concept of 'circulating capital' was used to obfuscate what was, in fact, due to the interdependence of labour. Thus labour was beholden to labour not capital and, in consequence, the profit on circulating capital represented exploitation not legitimate recompense.

Also, as regards fixed capital, 'it is the hand knowledge of the labourer which makes it, preserves it from decay, and which uses it to any beneficial end'. So, for Hodgskin, 'he who neither makes nor uses [it] has no just claim to any portion of the produce'.[13] Profit deriving from this source must also be seen, therefore, as an exaction rather than a just reward. It followed then, as regards both circulating and fixed capital, that 'profit is *derived ... from the power which the capitalist has over the labourer who consumes the circulating and uses the fixed capital*'. Or, as Hodgskin phrased it in *Popular Political Economy*, 1827: 'the individual capitalist did not grow rich by an actual and material saving, but by doing something which enabled him, according to some conventional usage, to obtain more of the produce of other men's labour'.[14] As a contemporary, J. Lalor, wrote, *Labour Defended* 'requires notice as containing the first clear conception of capital as mere *power*'.[15]

The material interests of the capitalist and the labourer were, therefore, necessarily antagonistic. Where political economists such as Smith, Ricardo and McCulloch emphasised the favourable impact that the rapid accumulation of capital would have on the demand for and thence real wages of labour, Hodgskin stressed that an increase in profits could only occur at the expense of the labouring class. As he phrased it in *Labour Defended*, 'wages vary inversely as profits; or wages rise when profits fall, and profits rise when wages fall; and it is therefore profits, or the capitalist's share of the national produce which is opposed to wages or the share of the labourer'.[16] It was this inverse relationship between profits and wages which formed the economic basis of that class antagonism which Hodgskin clearly saw as the dominant feature of early nineteenth century British society.

It is difficult, therefore, to go along with the view of Stedman Jones, who has argued that Hodgskin's 'focus on capital and capitalists neither disturbed basic radical assumptions, nor sanctioned a class hostility towards the employer, but rather, if anything, reinforced hostility to the traditional radical foes, the landlords and the moneylords'.[17] Clearly, the landlords were not the main object of Hodgskin's critical attack and the 'moneylords', at least as that economic category was understood by radicals, cannot be seen as being synonymous, as Stedman Jones would have it, with Hodgskin's 'capitalist'. For a radical such as Cobbett the 'moneylord' was someone who had grown rich from the buying or selling of government debt and/or from the paper money system which had emerged after 1797. For the Hodgskin of *Labour Defended*, the capitalist was someone whose exactions from labour derived from his 'power ... over the labourer who consumes the circulating and uses the fixed capital'.[18] Hodgskin's theory of exploitation and the understanding of social antagonism which he derived from it was, therefore, grounded in a distinction between those who owned and those who did not own the means of production. In that respect, and others, it represented a distinct break from the radical explanation of labour's impoverishment.[19]

It is true that Hodgskin uses the term 'interest' interchangeably
with 'profit' and it has been argued that this is indicative of the
extent to which there is a continuity between the critical analysis
of Hodgskin and that of political radicals like Cobbett. It was after
all the interest derived by fundholders from their purchase of
government debt which was at the root of the corruption which
Cobbett pilloried. And in relation to the exploitation of labour,
Hodgskin wrote that 'for the labourer to have ... articles he must
give over and above the quantity of labour nature demands from
him, a still larger quantity to the capitalist ... *he must pay
interest*'.[20] But Hodgskin also made evident the distinction
between his use of the concept of 'interest' and the use to which
it was put by the radicals. For 'what the capitalist really puts out
to interest ... is not gold or money, but food, clothing and instruments'.[21] Here again Hodgskin makes abundantly clear that what
generates interest/profit for the capitalist is not what generates
interest for the fundholder. It is not money and the manipulation
of the monetary system but the ownership of (circulating) capital
which is decisive.

There are also those who have made much of Hodgskin's use
of the term 'middleman' when describing the capitalist. Again,
the argument is that he conceived of the capitalist, in traditional,
radical fashion, as someone intervening in the marketplace in a
manner similar to that of forestallers and regraters, to secure
unmerited rewards and thereby undermine the basis of the moral
economy. Following on from this, it has been argued that because
Hodgskin conceived of exploitation and the hostility between
capitalists and labourers in such a manner, his view of things was,
again, not decidedly different from those radicals whose critique
of economic arrangements was rooted in a conception of an
endangered moral economy. In this reading, the crucial conflict
identified by Hodgskin was not that between capitalist master and
wage labourer but that between masters and men (taken together)
and those who used financial, monopoly and political power to
corrupt the business of buying and selling. It is such a view of
things that has led Joyce to claim that 'what early nineteenth
century radicals like Thomas Hodgskin pointed to was not a
picture of two opposed classes thrown up by a new system of
production but rather a harmonious world of production inhabited by master and man' and jeopardised by the malign activities
of those few who refused to play by the customary rules of the
market game. For similar reasons Stedman Jones has argued that
'Hodgskin's conception of "capitalist" exploitation ha[d] nothing
specific to say about the form of exploitation associated with
industrial capitalism' and that what he had in mind was 'a harmonious world of production inhabited by masters and men,

degraded by the artificial imposition of a political system which sanctions and sustains the extraction of exorbitant interest payments to a purely parasitic class of capitalists who garrison every point of exchange'.[22] Similarly, the author of a recent intellectual biography of Thomas Hodgskin has written that he 'did not analyse a specifically *industrial* form of capitalism' and that his was 'a pre-industrial analysis, of use *only to artisans, mechanics and other simple commodity producers*'[!][23]

But this is a misreading of Hodgskin. It is true, of course, that Hodgskin did frequently write of the capitalist as a middleman.

> Betwixt him who produces food and him who produces clothing, betwixt him who makes instruments and him who uses them, in steps the capitalist, who neither makes nor uses them, and appropriates to himself the produce of both. With as niggard a hand as possible he transfers to each a part of the produce of the other, keeping to himself the larger share. Gradually and successively has he insinuated himself betwixt them expanding in bulk as he has been nourished by their increasingly productive labours ... He is the middleman of all labourers.[24]

But note that the 'middleman' plays his role in relation to his ownership/provision of fixed (instruments) and circulating (food) capital; that is why he is denominated a capitalist and not simply a middleman. Whereas the role of the middleman had previously been conceived of in terms of the buying and selling of commodities, e.g. the forestalling and regrating of grain, Hodgskin stretched the concept to encompass the owners and providers of fixed and circulating capital. In Hodgskin's political economy the term therefore clearly acquires a dimension, indeed a class dimension, which it did not possess when deployed by those who thought in terms of a moral economy. The capitalist asserts his power not as a monopoliser of commodities, but as a possessor of the fixed and circulating means of production.

There is, though, this element of truth in these writers' reading of Hodgskin as depicting 'a harmonious world of production inhabited by master and man'. For Hodgskin the interests of the master manufacturer and journeyman labourer were not opposed. The master craftsman received a greater reward for his labour than those under his tutelage but, for Hodgskin, that was right and proper. However, Hodgskin was aware of the changing nature of the relationship between master and men as a consequence of the economic developments noted in Chapter 3. Masters were, in many instances, and in many trades, assuming the role of small capitalists and were moved by different imperatives and motives from what had previously been the case. The customs of the craft or trade now counted for less than the exaction of profit and power derived not from the knowledge and exercise of specific skills but from a control over fixed and circulating capital. Hodgskin wrote in this way about what he saw as the contemporary relationship between master and man.

> Masters, it is evident are labourers as well as journeymen. In this character their interest is precisely the same as that of their men. But they are also either capitalists or the agents of the capitalist, and in this respect their interest is decidedly opposed to the interest of their workmen ... The labourer should know and bear this in mind. Other people should also remember it, for it is indispensable to correct reasoning to distinguish between these two characters of the masters.[25]

In so far as they retained their former character, a harmonious world of production was possible. Hodgskin was quite clear that the productive part played by the master manufacturer was a vital one; both in his role of craftsman and also with respect to the entrepreneurial and organisational functions which he performed.

> The knowledge and skill of the master manufacturer, or of the man who plans and arranges a productive operation, who must know the state of the market and the qualities of different materials, and who has some tact in buying and selling, are just as necessary for the complete success of any complicated operation as the skill of the workmen.[26]

But, increasingly, the master manufacturer was ceasing to be just a superior labourer and, in consequence, the relationship between master and man was assuming a qualitatively different form. As we have seen, contemporary economic developments meant that the master craftsman in, for example, his subcontracting role, was increasingly becoming a small capitalist and/or a capitalist's agent.[27] His control over the fixed and circulating means of production was being used to buy sweated labour cheap and sell its products dear. In Hodgskin's words he was using his power over capital to transmute natural value into social price and thereby exploit the labourer. Where this occurred, as it increasingly did, the interests of master and man were necessarily opposed. Thus contemporary developments were, in large measure, destroying the possibility of a harmonious world of production; social harmony was being replaced by a necessary social antagonism where those in possession of the fixed and circulating means of production confronted those with only their labour power to sell and where transactions in the labour market assumed the form of a zero sum game with wages and profits inversely related.

This was the theory of labour exploitation which Hodgskin formulated. It was one which was consistent with developments occurring in the early nineteenth-century British *industrial* economy and it was one that was fundamentally different from that which had previously characterised the radical tradition. Hodgskin's analysis was pre-industrial only if one adheres to the now defunct notion that early nineteenth-century industrialisation was about the growth of the factory system. If, as Stack argues, his political economy was '*only*' applicable to artisans, mechanics and other simple commodity producers, that is to admit that it was applicable to a substantial component of the industrial workforce that existed in early nineteenth-century Britain.

It was because of Hodgskin's conception of the economic roots of social disharmony and antagonism that he supported the repeal of the Combination Acts and the formation of trade unions to defend the interests of labour. That indeed was the purpose of *Labour Defended,* which was written, significantly, in the aftermath of that repeal and the wave of trade union agitation it precipitated. Trade unions would counterpose the organised power of labour to that which derived from the ownership of capital'. They were 'practical attacks on the claims of capital'. The implication too was that the power of the capitalist had to be combatted in the economic sphere; it was to trade unions that Hodgskin looked to eliminate profits and secure the whole product of labour. 'The most successful and widest-spread possible combination to obtain an augmentation of wages would ... reduce the incomes of those who live on profit and interest, and who have no just claim but custom to any share of the national produce.'[28] Trade unions were therefore necessary organisations in the war against capital and would remain necessary so long as the conflict between capital and labour remained unresolved; a conflict in which there could be no social mediators and which must, ultimately, be decided by *force majeure.* As Hodgskin wrote: 'the capitalists and labourers form the great majority of the nation, so that there is no third power to intervene betwixt them. They must and will decide the dispute of themselves.'[29]

If the reading of Hodgskin by both Joyce and Stedman Jones is wrong in the ways suggested, it is also wrong in relation to another fundamental aspect of his anti-capitalist political economy and that is his understanding of the part played in the impoverishment of labour by political and legal structures. For Stedman Jones, who insists on the continuity between

Hodgskinian political economy and that of the radical tradition, Hodgskin is seen as locating the roots of exploitation in the political sphere. Thus, for Hodgskin, 'the source of unequal exchange was to be sought not in the economic process itself, but in artificial laws and political power'; similarly, 'the capitalist, through his control of the law, pockets all the increase in productivity for himself, and gives to the labourer no more than a subsistence wage' and, again, 'it was only in their role as middlemen, possessing a *political monopoly* over the exchange system, that they were to be opposed as capitalists'.[30]

Now Hodgskin, if anti-capitalist, was also an economic libertarian fundamentally influenced, as has been noted, by the deism of William Paley and by what he took to be Adam Smith's view of the economic world as a system of natural harmony, where individuals left free to pursue their material self-interest promoted the interests of all. As Hodgskin saw it, 'the whole system of social production must be considered ... as part of the universe, which man may observe and know *but cannot regulate*'.[31] He was also adamant that when governments had sought to regulate the economic system it was in ways that violated those laws, both effecting a maldistribution of wealth and obstructing the nation's subsequent economic development. Governments were also seen by Hodgskin as acting to appropriate for their own use, and that of their minions, a part of the wealth which labour produced. In that respect it is true that Hodgskin saw labour's ills as, in some measure, a direct consequence of the state's intervention in the economic life of the nation. In a manner reminiscent of Cobbett, for example, he argued that paper money was never issued by government 'but for the purpose of surreptitiously and fraudulently levying a tax on the people'. More generally, he stated that 'those who make laws appropriate wealth in order to secure power'. Tax and tithe gatherers along with 'paper money men' certainly figured in Hodgskin's demonology.[32]

Yet even in a work as concerned with an analysis of the state's violation of natural economic laws as *The Natural and Artificial Rights of Property Contrasted*, 1832, and in which governments were particularly portrayed as the progenitors of economic evil, it is still clear who Hodgskin saw as the primary perpetrators and beneficiaries of the contemporary maldistribution of wealth. 'At present', he wrote, 'all the wealth of society goes first into the possession of the capitalist and even most of the land has been purchased by him; he pays the landowner his rent, the labourer his wages, the tax and the tithe gatherer their claims, and *keeps a large, indeed the largest, and a continually augmenting share for himself*.'[33] So here the tax and tithe gatherers are seen as subsidiary parasites, not the primary cause of the impoverishment of labour. That accolade was clearly reserved for the capitalist and, as we have seen, the capitalist's power derived, by definition, from his ownership of fixed and circulating capital. It was, in effect, economic not political.

As to legislative interference in the working of the economy, that could certainly retard the expansion of wealth but it was detrimental primarily in so far as 'law *supported* an unjust appropriation of wealth'.[34] It was the legal *confirmation* and *defence* of the capitalist's artificial right to property which Hodgskin condemned, but that property originated not through the exercise of legislative but economic power. As Hodgskin wrote: 'the capitalist as such ... has no natural right to the large share of the annual produce *the law secures* to him'. Further, he wrote of 'the law' being 'extremely punctilious in *defending* the claims and exactions of the capitalists'.[35] Political power confirmed, supported and defended what the capitalist class had acquired, but capitalists acquired it through the exploitative use of the economic power which capital gave them. Further, in *Labour Defended* Hodgskin was clear that political power derived from economic power, not vice versa. Thus capital 'for its own security *added honour and political power* to wealth'.[36]

The primacy of the economic over the political in Hodgskin's anti-capitalist political economy can also be seen in his understanding of the relation between the distribution of wealth and both political systems and political behaviour. Thus in *The Natural and Artificial Rights of Property Contrasted* he wrote that 'political organisation depend[ed] very much on the mode in which property is distributed'. Also, in the same work, he insisted that the 'contest to obtain wealth' was invariably at the root of political disturbances and class dissensions. Again the economic sphere is seen as determining the political.[37]

Hodgskin's political economy goaded the popularisers of classical political economy to a vituperative response – something that again suggests he was doing more than simply amplifying the sentiments of political radicalism. Classical writers could accommodate a political economy that stressed the pernicious nature of state economic intervention but not one that called into question the nature of capital, the benefits of capital accumulation and the legitimacy of profits. James Mill railed against ideas which 'if they were spread ... would be the subversion of civilised society, worse than the overwhelming deluge of Huns and Tartars'. Similarly the Society for the Diffusion of Useful Knowledge, an organisation purveying classical political economy in popularised form, saw the notion of labour's right to the whole product as pointing back to a savage state where the 'ministers of desolation would be able to sing their triumphant song of "Labour defended against the

Claims of Capital" amid the shriek of the jackal and the howl of the wolf'.[38]

However, while Hodgskin's ideas provoked those who wished to stress the essential harmony of the interests of capital and labour, it is difficult to gauge the extent of Hodgskin's positive influence. Certainly there were aspects of his political economy which were appealing to elements of the labour movements which were emerging in the 1820s and 1830s and his work was noted by the working-class press of the period. Substantial excerpts from *Labour Defended* appeared in the *Trades' Newspaper*, a paper published in the 1820s by representatives of some London and provincial trades, while parts of the same work found their way into the *Destructive and People's Conservative*, 1833–34, a working-class paper edited by Bronterre O'Brien with a circulation of about 8,000. Passages from *Popular Political Economy* were reproduced in the *Lancashire and Yorkshire Co-operator*, 1831–32, and *The Natural and Artificial Rights of Property Contrasted* was quoted extensively in the *Poor Man's Guardian*, 1831–35, which, with a circulation peaking at 15,000, was one of the most popular working-class papers of the early nineteenth century. So Hodgskin's work may have helped to fuel and inform that working-class interest in political economy which was particularly evident in the 1820s and 1830s.

From the 1830s onwards Hodgskin's literary output took a journalistic form[39] with editorials, articles and reviews published in a series of papers aimed, primarily, at a middle-class audience. Such papers included the *Sun*, the *Courier*, the *Daily News*, the *Illustrated London News*, the *Brighton Guardian*, the *London Telegraph* and the *Economist*, with substantial contributions being made to the last three.[40] Throughout he adhered to the notion of a natural order whose essential harmony was only jeopardised by malign or, simply, unthinking interference. However, while there was no change in the philosophical fundamentals of his thought, the period after 1830 did see an alteration in certain aspects of his political economy. To begin with there was a strong emphasis on the manifold benefits to be derived from free trade and in particular a free trade in corn. In January 1843 he delivered a *Lecture on Free Trade in Connexion with the Corn Laws* and, at this time, he was certainly more sympathetic to the Anti-Corn Law League than he was to the Chartists. After all, the Chartists were in favour of interference by a reformed parliament to right the wrongs of labour and for Hodgskin that was anathema to his dogmatic *laissez-faire*. Hodgskin even opposed interference by the state to enhance working-class educational provision and was dismissive of the idea of factory legislation improving working conditions and shortening hours.

Also, in his journalistic output, there was a definite dilution of his anti-capitalism. The existence of a necessary antagonism between capitalists and labourers was increasingly disputed and, indeed, in the *Economist*, and elsewhere, he became critical of the activities of trade unions. More and more the theme developed was that of the unity of the labouring and middle classes, with the landowners coming to assume pride of place in the Hodgskinian demonology; particularly as regards their support of agricultural protection. One can only speculate as to the reasons for this shift in position. The need to market his literary skills in middle-class newspapers and periodicals, the strong and unambiguous support of the middle classes and middle-class papers for the free trade principles to which he had consistently adhered and, also, antipathy to the means, such as Chartism, by which the working class were pursuing their goals in the 1840s, may all have played a part. It may also have been the case that Hodgskin's anti-capitalism was eroded as capitalism itself changed and evinced a capacity to accommodate some, at least, of the material aspirations of labour. Whatever the reason Hodgskin's career as an anti-capitalist economist can be said to have been effectively over by the early 1830s.

Marx thought highly of *Labour Defended*. 'Here at last the nature of capital is understood correctly', he wrote in his *Theories of Surplus Value*.[41] But, even as regards his theory of exploitation, it would be wrong to see Hodgskin as Marx's precursor. Specifically it must be stressed that while Marx saw exploitation as taking place at the point of production, Hodgskin located it in the sphere of exchange. While Marx looked therefore to social ownership of the means of production as a solution to labour's impoverishment, Hodgskin looked to a vigorous trade unionism as a means of ensuring that labour secured the right to its whole product. His vision of the economically just society was, essentially, an individualistic and bourgeois one; a utopia founded upon a right to private property which was properly grounded in labour and where all received their full rights as the buyers and sellers of commodities. His writing in the 1820s provided a penetrating critique of contemporary capitalism of a kind which reflected the experience of, in particular, the artisanate involved in the London and provincial trades. It was anti-capitalist but not socialist and, in fact, Hodgskin never doubted the virtues, material and social, that emanated from the maintenance of private property. What he insisted on was that the right to private property must be founded in labour.

However, a fundamentally different view of how the position of the working class might be radically improved, and the iniquities and inequities of early nineteenth-century British capitalism obliterated, was to be provided by others who sought, in this period, to formulate a political economy that articulated the experience and advanced the interests of the working class. It is to the work of two such writers – Robert Owen and William Thompson – that we now turn.

CHAPTER 6

Communitarian Political Economy: Robert Owen and William Thompson

Born in Newtown, Montgomeryshire, in 1771, Robert Owen made his fortune as a cotton manufacturer before turning his attention to social reform. The opportunity to combine the one with the other came, in 1797, when he entered into partnership with David Dale and began to manage the New Lanark mills in Scotland. Proceeding from the premise that the character of human kind was formed for it not by it,[1] he sought to create at New Lanark a humanised working environment which would, in microcosm, effect a moral and social transformation of the work-force. His success, in terms of the marked improvement in their conduct and character, brought Owen to public prominence and New Lanark became a place of pilgrimage for those who sought the means by which to effect a fundamental improvement in the minds and morals of the working class.

Owen's thinking was, however, to take him in the direction of more radical expedients than that of simply transforming work-place conditions. Impoverishment and depravity, he came to believe, were not simply the consequence of a particular working environment; they were a product of a society which rested on an economic basis that was fundamentally flawed and manifestly inequitable. It was, therefore, the nature of the defects in contemporary competitive capitalism that Owen sought to identify in his political economy, as a necessary critical prelude to elucidating the means by which society might be transformed.

As a cotton manufacturer Owen grasped the profound material consequences and colossal productive potential of mechanisation. At the same time he was only too aware of the acute economic distress which followed the end of the Napoleonic Wars. Existing society was, therefore, clearly suffering the paradoxical affliction of 'pining in want amidst a superabundance'.[2]

Owen recognised, as did many contemporaries, that the diminution in government demand which followed the cessation of hostilities was a causal factor.[3] But he saw too that the deficiency of demand in relation to expanded supply had deeper roots. Working-class impoverishment was itself a cause of economic depression and, for Owen, could be linked to the expansion of mechanical power in an atomistic economic system which functioned according to competitive principles. Machinery had created 'a most unfavourable disproportion between the demand for and supply of manual labour; and in its daily undirected progress this disproportion will go on increasing'. Where, therefore, the remuneration of labour was dictated by 'the artificial law of supply and demand, arising from the principles of individual gain', competitive market forces would reduce wages to subsistence level.[4] As the remuneration of labour represented a substantial component of aggregate demand, glutted markets and a general redundancy of labour must ensue.

To tackle this state of affairs Owen suggested a number of palliatives and, with growing emphasis, one remedy. In *A New View of Society*, 1816, he put forward the idea of a national plan of employment giving the government responsibility for 'preparing a reserve of employment for the surplus working classes, when the general demand for labour throughout the country is not equal to the full occupation of the whole'.[5] Here the aim was both to provide remunerative occupation and to eliminate the downward pressure on wages exerted by redundant labour.

In addition, in a *Report to the County of Lanark*, 1821, 'one of the measures' which he 'venture[d] to propose to let prosperity loose on the country ... [was] a change in the standard of value'. Thus, as he saw it, 'the natural standard of value' was 'human labour' and to the extent that that standard prevailed, labour would be valued according to its contribution to production, rather than devalued by the forces of supply and demand.[6] Further, where goods were valued according to the labour time they contained and labour was valued according to the time it expended on production, demand would be made commensurate with supply and glutted markets and redundant labour would cease to exist.[7] There would then be no barrier 'to increasing to an unlimited extent, our scientific powers of production'. Such views were ultimately to be given practical expression in the so-called 'equitable labour exchanges' established in London, Birmingham and elsewhere in the early 1830s[8] and they represent one expression of that concern with the volatility of value which was a feature of anti-capitalist and socialist political economy in the immediate post-war period.

However, central to Owen's prescriptive thinking was the idea of 'villages of unity and mutual co-operation'. These would allow their denizens to furnish the greater part of their own subsistence and to use for social benefit those productive techniques that, in competitive circumstances, had precipitated their impoverish-ment. In addition, by removing the surplus from the labour market they would have the same salutary effect on wages as the national plan of employment. From this was to grow the idea of a self-sufficient co-operative community which, in addition to its economic advantages, would provide a microcosm free from the degenerate social behaviour and immorality which characterised contemporary Britain. It would, in effect, furnish the basis for the emergence of a new moral world. These would be 'permanent asylums which will for ever place us beyond the influence of the distressing cares and anxieties which are now periodically arriving'[9] but more than that they would foster a spirit of co-oper-ation and a sense of human interdependency which would banish the social antagonism, depravity and angst which were the inevitable concomitant of a possessive, competitive individualism.

With Owen, therefore, we have the birth, in Britain, of a communitarian socialist political economy. Yet it was a commu-nitarian socialism based on an analysis of the evils of early industrial capitalism which differed in important respects from that of many other, later, communitarian writers, even those who were to derive inspiration from Owen's work. There is, for example, no theory of labour exploitation in Owen's political economy. Engels wrote that 'English socialism arose with Owen, a manufacturer, and proceeds, therefore, with great consideration towards the bourgeoisie'.[10] With respect to Owen himself, this aphorism contains a measure of truth. In *A New View of Society*, Owen described himself as 'a manufacturer for pecuniary profit' and he clearly saw a certain level of profits as legitimate.[11] In seeking to establish his villages he looked, initially, to support from potential investors and to these he promised that such estab-lishments would not only remoralise the population employed, but also 'return 5% interest for the capital expended'.[12] Not only would labourers be enabled 'to consume a larger proportion than heretofore, of that which they produce', but 'the higher ranks of society [will receive] a much larger surplus than they have yet received from the working classes'.[13] We also find him writing, in his autobiography, of a Mr McGuffog who 'would have a *reason-able* profit upon what he sold', with the clear implication that the idea of a 'reasonable' profit was a defensible concept.[14]

More importantly, in terms of explaining this absence of a theory of exploitation, Owen tended to see the impoverishment of labour as the product of ignorance and systemic failure rather than the avaricious and consciously malign use of economic power. There was ignorance as to how society might best use the rapidly expanding powers of production available to it; ignorance of where need lay and how it might best be satisfied; ignorance as to how demand and supply might be matched. The essence of the systemic failure was the reliance on untrammelled competition as the motive and organising force of economic activity. It was this that prevented the labouring class 'from producing more than a very small part ... of the real wealth which your present skill and industry rightly directed, would enable you to bring into existence'.[15]

Such a view of the causes of impoverishment ruled out the formulation of a theory of exploitation. The poor were poor not because they were exploited but because economic ignorance and economic anarchy denied humanity access to that abundance which was within its grasp. There was no need to identify the beneficiaries of labour's impoverishment, the source of their exploitative power, the way in which that power was wielded and the manner in which it could be most effectively attenuated or destroyed. The best antidote to ignorance was general enlightenment as to the advantages of co-operation; the solution to the systemic failure of an economy organised on competitive lines was the formation of co-operative communities. As to existing accumulations of capital these could be neglected as being of little importance. Apart from anything else, within their confines, co-operative communities would realise humanity's capacity to create abundance, so rendering existing concentrations of wealth unimportant and the power to be derived from them nugatory. Thus co-operative communities would eliminate the causes of misery 'without entering into contest with them [i.e. the capitalist and landowner], without infringing on any imaginary privileges which prior circumstances have placed in their hands'.[16] There is, therefore, in the political economy of Owen, neither the formulation, nor the need for the formulation, of a theory of labour exploitation nor an associated conception of class antagonism. When Owen did write of the social antagonism engendered by existing economic arrangements, it was in terms of the war of all, against all, not class against class. It was, in the final analysis, 'the system of *individual* opposing interest' which he condemned.

Rather than class antagonism, it was the potential harmony of interests which Owen constantly stressed. For example, those expedients that, while falling short of co-operative communities, would none the less raise the wages of labour were seen as being very much in the interest of capitalist employers because 'no evil ought to be more dreaded by the master manufacturers than low wages of labour ... These, in consequence of their numbers, are the greatest consumers of all articles.'[17] Villages of mutual co-operation should also be welcomed by all because they would raise a degraded labour force which might otherwise pose a threat to property and because they provided an opportunity for labourers 'to create all their own subsistence *and repay the interest of all the capital invested in the outfit of the establishment'*.[18] As noted above, Owen expected that these villages would raise the living standards of both the labouring class and 'the higher ranks of society'. It is not surprising, therefore, that he should articulate the view that 'the rich and the poor, the governors and the governed have really but one interest'.[19]

However, other writers, and in particular William Thompson, were to provide communitarian socialism with a political economy more fundamentally critical of early nineteenth-century industrial capitalism and its protagonists. Thompson was born in Cork in 1775. His grandfather was a Protestant clergyman and his father a wealthy Cork merchant who became speaker and mayor of the municipality and later High Sheriff of the County. On the death of his father in 1814, he took over the management of the family's mercantile interests and, in addition, inherited an estate of some 1,400 acres near Glandore in County Cork.

Thompson displayed an early interest in ideas of social improvement. He read the works of Godwin and Bentham and was exposed to the influence of continental writers such as Sismondi and St Simon during a period spent in France and the Low Countries. It was, no doubt, the articulation of the views of these writers that led to his being branded locally a 'Red Republican', a radical reputation further enhanced by his support for a candidate favouring Catholic Emancipation in the elections of 1812 and 1826 and his championing of popular education in a pamphlet entitled *Practical Education for the South of Ireland,* which was published in 1818.

Thompson's concern with the iniquities of existing economic and social arrangements was also made apparent, though in a more practical manner, when he took over his estate at Glandore. In Ireland these arrangements were frequently characterised by absentee landlords, rapacious rack-renting agents, evictions and, as a result, a poverty-stricken and disaffected peasantry. In contrast to much contemporary practice, Thompson took an interest in his estate, giving his tenants long leases on favourable terms, encouraging the introduction of improved agricultural techniques and establishing a model farm to illustrate best practice.

In 1819 he was invited by Bentham, with whom he had corresponded on educational questions, to visit him at his home in Queen Square Place, Westminster. He accepted, staying with him from October 1822 until February 1823. Here he met some of the leading utilitarians and political economists of the period, including Robert Torrens, James Mill, John Black (editor of the *Morning Chronicle*) and John Bowring (editor of the *Westminster*

Review). Such figures undoubtedly had a profound impact on a mind which, on educational theory, had already proved susceptible to Benthamite ideas. Thus Thompson wrote of Bentham in 1824 that he 'had done more for moral science than Bacon did for physical science'.[20]

Yet, at this time, the socialist ideas of Robert Owen were also leaving their mark on Thompson's thought, leading him to consider, in a different light, the material evils inflicted by the existing economic and social order and, specifically, the reasons for the inequitable distribution of wealth which characterised it.[21] The fruit of this was the classic text of communitarian political economy, *An Inquiry into the Principles of the Distribution of Wealth*, which was published in 1824. G.J. Holyoake wrote of it that it required 'a sense of duty to read ... curiosity is not sufficient'[22] and indeed, it is a long and at times tediously repetitive work whose difficulty is exacerbated by an opaque and convoluted prose style which tries the patience of even the sympathetic reader. To get to grips with it, it helps, at the outset, to grasp the central question which the work addressed because that dictated both its structure and the development of Thompson's argument. That question was whether economic and social arrangements might be devised which would allow a reconciliation of the socialist principle of equality with the Benthamite principle of security of possession. Under existing arrangements both were violated. As Thompson saw it, those who laboured *should* be secure in the possession of what their labour produced. 'Labour [was] the sole parent of wealth'[23] but as the victim of 'force and fraud' it received but a fraction of its product. The primary perpetrators of this spoilation were the government and the owners of land and capital. It was they who were the violators of the principle of security or, phrased differently, of the right of labour to his whole product. So while Robert Owen tended to explain labour's impoverishment by reference to the operations of a perniciously competitive economic system, Thompson explained it in terms of the exploitative actions of 'public and private plunderers' within that system. This explanation involved two things, both of which distinguished Thompson from Owen. First, it led Thompson to formulate a theory of labour exploitation, and second, to give much greater consideration than Owen had to the political causes of labour's destitution.

In the first part of the *Inquiry* Thompson considered both the violations of the principle of security and the extent to which they could be eliminated under the existing 'competitive system'. Here there is considerable emphasis on the 'public plunder' resulting from taxation, the granting of monopolies, wage regulation, bounties, tariffs, tithes, etc. This 'abstraction by political power of the products of labour without the consent of the producers or owners of them' was 'more extensive, more difficult of cure, and consequently more pernicious than PRIVATE plunder'.[24] It was 'to the wholesale violations of security by rulers that the poverty of communities are chiefly owing'. Further, against such depredations there were few means of defence. In so far as Thompson did hazard a solution, it was that of more 'representative government', which would act to eliminate those legislative and other political restraints on freedom of economic action and those violations of secure possession which directly impoverished productive labour.[25]

Thus there is in Thompson's *Inquiry* much that is redolent of late eighteenth- and early nineteenth-century political radicalism.[26] Here the influence of Bentham, James Mill and others is apparent. Yet while the cause of much of labour's exploitation is political, Thompson also considered the nature of private plunder and the power which made it possible, and in doing so he began to distance himself, in some measure, from political radicalism and classical political economy. Here Thompson noticed the economic power conferred by land, but also that which derived from the ownership of capital. Capital is defined as 'that part of the products of labour which, whether of a permanent nature or not, is capable of being made the instrument of profit'.[27] For Thompson that profit derived from the power of the capitalist to effect unequal exchanges with those who had only their labour to offer for sale.

> The capitalist getting into his hands, under the reign of insecurity and force, the consumption of many labourers for the coming year, the tools or machinery necessary to make their labour productive and the dwellings in which they must live, turned them to the best account, and bought labour and its future products with them as cheaply as possible. The greater the profit of capital or the more the capitalist made the labourer pay for the advance of his food, the use of the implements or machinery ... the less of course remained to the laborer for the acquisition of any other object of desire.[28]

For Thompson the magnitude of this power and thence the rate of the profit were determined by the distribution of capital. Thus 'the amount demanded for the use of capital depends more on the mode of its distribution than on the absolute quantity accumulated'.[29] So while classical economists might argue that a rapid rate of capital accumulation, outstripping the growth of the labour force, would raise wages and depress the rate of profit (the corollary being that labour's interest lay in the rapid accumulation of

capital), Thompson argued that what determined the rate of wages
was the extent to which capital, and the power it gave, was concentrated in the hands of few or many capitalists. Thus 'where all the
capital of the community is in the hands of men called capitalists
and scarcely any remains in the hands of the producers, there will
the price of the use of it be very high whether the absolute quantity
of capital be large or small, from ... the immense competition to
obtain the use of it.'[30] Further, with the ownership of capital
residing in a few hands the way was open for a

> universal and always vigilant conspiracy of capitalists ...
> founded on a universally existing interest to cause the
> labourers to toil for the lowest possible, and to wrest as much
> as possible of the products of their labour to swell the accu-
> mulations and expenditure of capitalists.[31]

Such was the case, as Thompson saw it, in early nineteenth-
century Britain.

This view of exploitation inevitably led Thompson on to
consider the economic interests of capitalist and labourer as antagonistic. Thus 'the real interest of the capitalist, as such, is always
and necessarily opposed to the interest of the labourer'. It was, as
he saw it, 'a self-evident proposition, that the higher the profits of
capital – other things remaining the same – the lower must be the
wages of labour'.[32] Thompson's conception of class antagonism
derived, therefore, from his perception of the nature of labour's
economic relationship to the owners of the means of production.

So while, in line with political radicalism, Thompson saw
government as a major source of the economic ills which labour
suffered, capitalists

> by means of the possession of this fixed, permanent or slowly
> consumed part of national wealth, of the land and materials to
> work upon, of tools to work with, the houses to shelter whilst
> working ... command for their own benefit the yearly produc-
> tive powers of all the really efficient productive labourers of
> society.[33]

Labour was exploited and labour would remain exploited as long
as it was separated from the means of production and the means
of subsistence.

> As long as the laborer stands in society divested of everything
> but the mere power of producing, as long as he possesses
> neither the tools nor the machinery to work with, the land or
> materials to work upon, the house and the clothes which

shelter him, or even the food which he is consuming in the act of producing; as long as any institutions or expedients exist, by the open or unseen operation of which he stands dependent, day by day, for his very life on those who have accumulated these necessary means of his exertions; so long will he remain deprived of almost all the products of his labour, instead of having the use of all of them.[34]

There is much here, of course, that prefigures the socialist political economy of later writers, yet the Thompson of the *Inquiry* developed his ideas on capitalist exploitation in a unique way and in a manner more reminiscent of the anti-capitalism of Hodgskin than the socialism of Owen, with whom he is so often linked. Thus, like Hodgskin, Thompson believed that unequal exchanges and the exploitation that eventuated represented a violation of the natural laws of distribution of which both public *and* private plunderers were guilty. In addition, he accepted that the depredations of both could be considerably reduced *without* resort to the kind of communitarian socialism which, none the less, he saw as the ideal to be pursued. As regards capitalist exploitation this might be done by a truly free competition both between capitalists and labourers and between capitalists themselves. Such competition would have a number of salutary consequences. It would raise the rate of wages as many competing capitalists would bid for the services of labour, and by the same token it would lower the rate of profit. It would also act as a constant check on the rate of profit, for if the demand for particular products was 'great and the profits keep high, new adventurers, where the law is not absurd enough to prevent it, spring up and break down the profits'.[35] Like the classical economists, therefore, Thompson was alive to the regulatory role which new entrants, or the threat of new entrants, had on the rate of profits, and his general view of the impact of capitalist competition on the rate of profits is strongly reminiscent of Adam Smith. Where true competition prevailed the natural laws of distribution would be operative; exchanges would be free and equal, commodities would exchange according to their labour value, labour itself would receive its whole product, the ownership of land and capital would be widely dispersed and that in turn would reinforce the competitive forces acting in the economy. Indeed, in the *Inquiry*, Thompson went so far as to state that 'when all obstacles of force and fraud to the entire development of free labour were removed', what resulted 'would approach ... very nearly to Mr. Owen's system of mutual co-operation by common labour'.[36] In effect a system of free labour and voluntary exchanges would, to a large extent, provide the economic equity and the material benefits which were claimed as the attributes of co-operative communities by their proponents, while at the same time vindicating the principle of security of possession. 'Thus we see that by means of the voluntary exchanges of labour or its products, we have a rule of action which reconciles and brings into harmonious operation the two principles of equality and security.'[37] There is much here that would have found favour with Thomas Hodgskin.

So why the need for the creation of co-operative communities if so much could be achieved in the context of a truly competitive capitalism, where the natural laws of distribution prevailed? To begin with, while free competition would make for greater equality it would not deliver the goal of equality itself. Only within a co-operative community, where all voluntarily relinquished the right to their whole product, could the principles of equality and security be finally reconciled. Second, while free labour and voluntary exchanges would deliver the greater part of the material benefits which co-operative communities would furnish, there were ineradicable social, psychological and ethical diseconomies which inhered to even the most truly competitive market. Thompson's discussion of these diseconomies was to be more fully developed in a later work, *Labor Rewarded*, 1827, but they were also touched on in the *Inquiry*. A society based on a competitive economy did nothing to ensure that women were freed from domestic subservience and their productive powers unleashed. The competitive economy itself was, inevitably, characterised by ignorance, miscalculation and the concealment of inventions which might be exploited for social benefit. In encouraging self-ishness, a competitive economy was also a progenitor of vice and crime. It engendered too an instrumental attitude to people with 'human beings themselves' being made 'articles of trade' and 'nothing in life [being] so sacred as not to find its price in money'.[38] Further, a competitive economy made no provision for the sick and the aged. Only within a co-operative community could such evils be removed.

In holding the views he did on what might be achieved, even in a competitive context, Thompson none the less distinguished himself from most communitarian socialists and certainly from Robert Owen. He also did so in another significant way. For, in line with his position on the importance of public plunder and the role played by the political system in supporting a system of forced exchanges and coerced labour, he discussed what political means might be used to alleviate labour's plight. Here he placed emphasis on the need for representative government. Such a government was necessary to remove legislative interference with the natural laws of distribution; it was therefore a prerequisite for the emergence of free labour and voluntary exchanges. Further, even though Thompson believed that a system of co-operative communities might be created independently of any alteration in the existing distribution of capital and land and that the new moral world of co-operative communities could grow within the womb of existing immoral arrangements, it was still the case that the continuation of public plunder could inhibit their development. For 'against the attacks on the security of the public plunderer, systematically organised and upheld ... there [were] no means of defence' even for co-operative communities. 'It [was] under free governments alone', therefore, 'that mutual co-operating communities [could] flourish'. In effect, for Thompson, political reform and the emergence of representative government was crucial to the growth and prosperity of communitarian socialism.[39]

The position which Thompson took up in *Labor Rewarded* was characterised by many of the elements of the *Inquiry*, but there were also a number of important differences. In particular there was Thompson's discussion of competition. The 1827 work was written as a critical response to Hodgskin's *Labour Defended* and it is not surprising, therefore, that in it Thompson should once again have discoursed at some length on free competition and the natural laws of distribution. Here, at a theoretical level, Thompson still acknowledged, if with greater qualification than before, the benefits that might accrue from 'truly free competition'.[40] But, in *Labor Rewarded*, Thompson discussed, in more extended fashion, the conditions that would have to be met if such competition were to exist. For Thompson such conditions were formidable. Free labour and voluntary exchanges could only be 'founded on equal means of knowledge and skill, on an equal command of the means of production, and on an equal freedom from all mental or physical restraints of law, superstition, or public opinion'. Elsewhere Thompson wrote that

to give fair scope to the real, *bona fide*, freedom of competition of all with all, not only ought all forcible taxation and unequal institutions to cease; not only ought equal education, equal means of knowledge and skill, to be afforded to all; but also all ought at birth, or at setting out in life, in the race of competition, to be made equal in the means of success depending on capital ... To render competition between the individuals of each successive generation equal, the children of all ought, at the common cost to be equally educated; and the fortunes of all should be equalized on beginning the race of competition.[41]

Clearly such conditions could not be easily met and certainly not in the foreseeable future. Further the competitive system itself was seen by Thompson, in 1827, as an 'insurmountable bar to this perfect freedom of labor and to this equal diffusion of knowledge'.[42]

In *Labor Rewarded*, therefore, truly free competition begins to assume all the characteristics of the unattainable. It was its proponents such as Hodgskin, not communitarian socialists like Owen, who trafficked in utopias. Even in the United States, 'where the most favourable specimen of the system of Individual Competition exists', 'chicane in the exchanges of commodities, or produce ... against each other in manufacturing and commercial industry, reigns supreme'.[43] The fact was that there was something in the very nature of the 'higgling of the market' that made for economic injustice. For 'the springs of the higgling will always be kept in the hands of the adepts, and they will be so regulated that prizes there will be, and those prizes will fall into the hands of the most skilful in the higgling exchanges of competition'.[44] The implication of all this, of course, was that co-operative communities, from which the competitive market was absent, were the only realistic means by which to secure what free competition purported to deliver.

In *Labour Rewarded*, Thompson's position on what might be expected from political reforms is consistent with this. As in the *Inquiry* he accepted that the creation of truly representative institutions would go some way to ameliorate the lot of labour. Certainly under the competitive system 'there [could] be no security from force and fraud, direct or indirect, till all laws are made by those whose interests they affect' and 'of all the expedients of competition for ameliorating the situation of mankind or of the Industrious Classes, this is by far the most efficient'. However, Thompson was equally clear that 'the grand measure of equal representative institutions will not necessarily, *nor even to any extent worth notice, while individual competition remains the principle of human exertion*, secure to the industrious classes the whole products of their labour'.[45] The fact was that political reforms could only go some limited way to purge the economic system of its exploitative characteristics. They could be used to eliminate 'loans and taxes forcibly levied by the Idle Classes on the Industrious Classes ... [and] experiments in coin-debasing or paper-currency', which were becoming 'everyday expedients of the law-making idle classes'.[46] They could, in part, ameliorate labour's sufferings, but they could not touch the (economic) root causes of exploitation and consequent working-class impoverishment. In short, traditional radical political expedients were not enough.

The industrious have been led to believe that were all these [forced taxes] removed, were the currency fixed and taxes removed, all would be well. That the industrious would derive some benefit ... there can be no doubt ... [but] Ignorance of the industrious, cunning of the idle, impotence of the industrious, power of the idle, hold on, with unrelenting Competition, their steady course; *till in a few years the laborers find that the capitalists ... have supplied the place of tax-gatherers, and that their situation remains radically the same.*[47]

As long as the existing competitive system prevailed, the power of capital would ensure that unequal exchanges would be an integral feature of economic life. For 'it [was] capital ... dexterous in the mere tricks and over-reaching of exchanges, in the turns of the market, that now wallow[ed] ... in enormously unequal shares of the national produce'. To create a *truly* competitive system was, as we have seen, impossible and certainly beyond the power of any legislature, however representative.[48] The fact was that whatever

multitudes of minor steps they may make to improve their present system; no great step can they make without stepping beyond their Competitive System ... that system necessarily associating comparative poverty with labor, affluence with idleness or pernicious activity, labor without capital, on the one hand, capital and knowledge commanding and enjoying the products of labor, on the other.[49]

This view of things underpinned the understanding of social antagonism which Thompson articulated in *Labor Rewarded*. For the labouring class, the *bête noir* of the radicals, the feudal aristocracy had still to be taken seriously as a social antagonist. 'It seems inaccurate to say', wrote Thompson, 'that the capitalist and moneyed aristocracy have supplanted in Britain the old feudal aristocracy, or inherited its power. Both species of aristocracy, the capitalist and the feudal, the old aristocracy of open force and the new aristocracy of chicane, have formed a coalition against the Industrious Classes'.[50] Nevertheless this should be set in the context of what he had to say about the increasing exactions of capitalists and the growing proportion of labour's product which they appropriated. Thompson undoubtedly saw the emergence of a growing social gulf between the capitalist and the labouring class and a growing consciousness within both classes of the distinct nature of their interests. As regards the capitalists' attitude to labour,

by the immensity of their acquisitions and the incidents of competition that they must have passed through in acquiring

> them ... [they] not only utterly los[e] all sympathy with the
> industrious, but ... acquire a sufficiently lordly antipathy to
> them ... as to forget any similarity of species with them.

As for the labouring class, trade unions, about whose economic
efficacy Thompson had considerable reservations, in 'extend[ing]
and comprehend[ing] different trades' led the labourer

> to embrace larger circles of the Industrious in his good wishes,
> till *he shall ultimately feel an interest in the happiness of all the
> Industrious*, agriculturists and day-laborers as well as
> mechanics, from *perceiving that the interests of all are the same.*[51]

For Thompson class consciousness and widening class divisions
were therefore a by-product of existing economic arrangements.

Neither the natural law, free market, anti-capitalism of
Hodgskin nor the nostra of the political radicals were sufficient to
remedy this state of affairs. As regards the latter, institutions
representative of the interests of labour might have the capacity to
facilitate the creation of co-operative communities,[52] but it was
only once such communities existed that the exploitation of
labour would cease. Only once the system of competitive
exchanges had been swept away could the inequalities which
derived from the coercive bargaining power of capital be eliminated. In short, the only effectual solution to labour's material ills
lay in a communitarian transformation of existing economic and
social arrangements.

Co-operative communities or, as Thompson termed them,
'communities of mutual co-operation' would, collectively, give
labour the ownership of capital necessary for productive
activity.[53] They would, therefore, allow labourers to withdraw
from the system of unequal exchanges where exploitation resulted
from the bargains struck with coercive capital. It was this that
would ensure that labour, collectively, secured the whole product
of its labour. The creation of autarchic or near autarchic co-operative communities[54] would eliminate the need to exchange and in
so doing remove the possibility of exploitation. For this reason
Thompson exhorted labourers to

> unite in large numbers ... supplying each other's wants. On
> land taken in a healthy situation, let some of you raise your
> own food, let others on that land raise your workhouses and
> dwellings, let others fabricate linen, woollen and cotton articles
> for your clothing, let others make up those and other articles
> for use, and let others prepare out of the raw materials the most
> useful articles of furniture, for the while; thus affording an

unfailing market to each other, and always equal supply and demand.[55]

Where communities wished to satisfy demands beyond their own productive capacity, they should, ideally, enter into exchange relations with other co-operative communities. But these exchanges would be conducted on the basis of labour for labour, thereby removing, it was believed, any possibility of being unequal. In effect the exchange relations between communities would be socialised. Further, where exchanges had to be conducted with 'society at large' it should only be for 'articles of rational desire', which 'they could not at all or without great loss of labour, fabricate themselves at home'.[56] However, the ideal was autarchy and, as that ideal was approached, so would the objective of labour collectively receiving its whole product. 'In proportion to the number of articles consumed by them, *which they produce and supply to each other*, will be the advance which they make towards the possession of the whole products of their labor.'[57]

Autarchic co-operative communities would also end the immorality and the social disharmony which were an ineradicable part of competitive exchange. Thus all market exchanges were in some measure at the 'expense of ... [the] truth, sincerity and benevolence of all engaged'. They involved the 'gratification of antipathy', they were productive of 'pain and evil' and, in particular, they 'eradicate[d] all feelings of benevolence'. To the extent that material life was conducted in the absence of market exchange, therefore, human behaviour and social relationships would be transformed and the basis laid for a new moral world.[58]

The impact of the political economy of Thompson, Owen and other Owenite writers was profound. As early as 1821 a group of London printers came together under the leadership of the Owenite George Mudie to form the Co-operative and Economical Society.[59] By 1823 this had failed, but a few years later, in 1825, the first Owenite community was established at Orbiston, near Motherwell, in Scotland, and the next 30 years saw, in Britain, the formation of another six Owenite communities and a number of communitarian experiments in which Owenites participated. Owen himself, convinced that a new moral world required a new world for its setting, sank half his fortune in the creation of New Harmony, Indiana, and in America some 16 Owenite or Owenite-influenced communities were created. All these communities, whether in Britain or the United States, were short-lived. Some, like Queenwood, near Tytherley, Hampshire, and that at New Harmony lasted a number of years; others survived for a much shorter period of time. Yet their very existence highlights the potency of the response which communitarian political economy evoked.[60]

So too do other developments in the 1820s and 1830s. To begin with these decades witnessed the growth of co-operative trading societies to a point where, by the early 1830s, there were over 300 in existence. It was 'Dr. William King of Brighton who joined Owenism to the co-operative store' with the founding of the Brighton Co-operative Benevolent Fund Association in 1827.[61] His objective, like most of the co-operative trading associations which were subsequently established, was to generate the capital necessary to establish a co-operative community. Along with these societies there also grew up organisations and means for the propagation of co-operative principles, such as the British Association for the Promotion of Co-operative Knowledge, 1829, and a burgeoning co-operative, working-class press – the *London Co-operative Magazine* (1826–30), the *Birmingham Co-operative Herald* (1828–30), the *Lancashire and Yorkshire Co-operator* (1831–32) and the *Herald to the Trades Advocate and Co-operative Journal* (1830–31) being among the more important papers.

Further, there was the establishment of labour exchanges which both sought to give practical expression to the principle that goods should exchange according to their labour value and also to provide a means of raising capital for the formation of communities. Thus while goods were to be valued in terms of labour time, there would be a percentage mark-up which would be accumulated for communitarian purposes. In the United States, Josiah Warren, a former member of the Owenite New Harmony community established a time store in Cincinnati in 1827.[62] But in Britain it was yet another William King who proved the pioneer, founding as he did a Union Exchange Society, 1827, where labourers met to exchange their products. This institution functioned without labour money but, in 1832, the First Western Union Exchange Bank and the Gothic Hall Labour Bank were created and made use of labour notes.[63] This was followed by the establishment of a National Equitable Labour Exchange, with which Owen was directly connected, and a Birmingham Equitable Labour Exchange, in whose creation Owenites such as William Pare and William Hawkes Smith were heavily involved. Though for a time seemingly successful, these institutions were, like the co-operative communities, short-lived. The range of products available for exchange was limited and there was a distinct absence of basic provisions for which labour notes could be exchanged. Further, the problems of valuing goods in terms of labour time meant that errors were made and, inevitably, there were goods undervalued in relation to their market equivalents that were quickly purchased, while there were others that were overvalued and just as rapidly accumulated in the exchanges. Only where the labour exchanges replicated the market valuation were there no such problems. In effect, therefore, market price rapidly exerted its hegemony over labour values.[64]

However, leaving aside these failures of practical socialism, it is important to consider just why and to whom they proved so powerfully appealing. For E.P. Thompson the potency of that appeal was as multifaceted as the experiments themselves. They proved attractive to

> artisans with their dreams of short-circuiting the market economy; the skilled workers with their thrust towards general unionism ... the poor with their dream of land or of Zion: the weavers with their hopes of self employment: and all of these with their image of an equitable brotherly community, in which mutual aid would replace aggression and competition.[65]

Yet even this does not exhaust the multiform nature and socially variegated response which practical communitarianism could evoke. For, above all, what communities offered was sanctuary: sanctuary from the vices attendant upon self-seeking competition, from the 'corroding anxiety and care' generated by an increasingly volatile economic world, from the 'restless discontent and disquietude' which the self-interested pursuit of gain engendered and from the social insecurity and economic depredations of early industrial capitalism.[66]

Communitarians could eschew the necessity of involuntary and unequal exchanges in marketless milieux and where exchange relations with others were necessary, they could be assured that these would be mediated by a labour currency. They were safe, therefore, from the coercive exercise of economic power and, to the extent that they became self-sufficient, that security became absolute. They were insulated too from the consequences of general economic depression and the fluctuations in the valuation of money which had been salient characteristics of the late eighteenth- and early nineteenth-century British economy. Communities also held out the prospect of independence and the social status and security which came with that. For those artisans and skilled workers threatened with an influx of cheap labour to their trades; whose trades had lost their 'honourable' status; who had become a sweated prey to middlemen and large-scale employers; who had seen the switchblade of the market pare customary prices and wages to a subsistence minimum and whose position had been undermined by technical and organisational change, the hope that communities would restore the basis of their self-determination gave them a powerful appeal. As to those involved in large-scale production, whose skill was negligible or had atrophied through their being shackled to one small fragment of the production process, communities held out the possibility of acquiring skill in a context where the excessive subdivision of labour did not prevail. There was also, for many, the prospect of material abundance and an end to the grinding material impoverishment which was integral to their experience of competitive capitalism.

It can be argued too that artisans and skilled labourers would have warmed to a political economy that had the labour theory of value as a central theoretical component. That theory was articulated in a variety of ways but the crucial point was that labour was the source of all wealth; it was the sole productive factor; its creativity was fundamental to the nation's economic prosperity. Where status was threatened, where the value of labour was depreciating, where labour was being displaced by machinery, where skills were rendered defunct and labour made 'dishonourable', this was a political economy that many would have found congenial. The nature of the threat which early industrial capitalism posed to the status of labour also explains, in some measure, the manifest support for labour exchanges. These were certainly attractive as the anteroom to the new moral world. But in their own right they suggested that if exchange were moralised/socialised, then the status and worth of the independent artisan or skilled labourer could, in fact, be restored.[67] For many they would have been seen as the practical articulation of the notions of moral economy.

The appeal of communitarian socialism must be seen too in terms of pre-existing traditions of working-class mutuality. The guilds, burial clubs, trade societies, friendly societies, trade unions of the eighteenth and early nineteenth centuries represented collective attempts to provide a measure of material security for those who, individually, were unlikely to survive the chill blast of the competitive economic wind.[68] Further, as one commentator has pointed out: 'co-operation, both of consumers and producers antedated Owenism. In the second half of the eighteenth century the dockyard workers of Woolwich and Chatham founded co-operative corn mills and there were similar ventures in Yorkshire. Co-operative storekeeping was pioneered in Scotland and the North of England from 1769 onwards.'[69] The tradition of collective, working-class self-help was therefore a powerful one; one into which communitarian socialism could tap while holding out the possibility of its fuller and more sophisticated expression and realisation. It was also the case that these early institutional expressions of working-class mutuality themselves generated a language of harmony, union and community which supplied the rhetorical building blocks of the socialist idiom.[70]

There can be little doubt either that the fact that communities were described and actually portrayed as essentially agrarian goes some way to explain the support that they received. Thus Owen wrote of 'a judicious arrangement of spade cultivation, *with manufactures as an appendage*' and of 'communities of individuals on the principle of united labour and expenditure *having their basis in agriculture*'.[71] Of course the goal of self-sufficiency dictated that they had to be primarily agricultural, but what was a necessity was also seen by many as a virtue, indeed *the* distinctive virtue of communities. For such individuals their appeal was not simply that they banished impoverishment and the coercive exercise of economic power, they also closed the door on what was seen as the moral and material squalor engendered by commercialism and urbanisation. Rural virtue was counterposed to urban vice. Here (and elsewhere) communitarian socialism tapped into pre-existing currents of thinking influential among the working class. The views of Spence, Ogilvie and Cobbett have already been noticed and, certainly, it was not unusual for Spenceans such as Allen Davenport to make the transition from the Land Plan to support for Owenite co-operative communities.[72] If dictated by expediency, therefore, the communitarian socialist emphasis on the advantages to be derived from an agrarian basis to society was one that was projected at an audience already familiar with and receptive to such notions.

As the political economy of Thomas Spence and its reception show, a hunger for land preceded communitarian socialism and, for that matter, was to survive its demise. As E.P. Thompson has phrased it, 'for the poor, Owenism touched one of their deepest responses – the dream that, somehow, by some miracle, they might once again have some stake in the land'.[73] It was also the case that in the early nineteenth century an industrial capitalist transformation of Britain had some considerable way to go and the ultimate triumph of industrialism over an agrarian economy did not have about it the aura of inevitability which it was to assume as the nineteenth century progressed. Other futures, other paths of economic development, seemed open; not least one based on the collective use of the nation's primary resource. What Engels with hindsight might stigmatise as utopian need not have appeared so when communities actually burgeoned in a Britain still predominantly rural. For some, indeed, the dream became a reality and for others that fact would have reinforced the belief that for them too it might become so.

Finally, the appeal of community lay also in its reconstitution of a moral economy. The withdrawal from the world represented not simply a retreat from 'the mass of outward deteriorating circumstances' but also from the 'falsehood, thieving, perjury', the 'envies, jealousies, ill-will, suspicions and dread of ill-offices from all around'. It involved the rejection of a system where 'all [were] sedulously trained to buy cheap and sell dear' and so were 'taught to acquire strong powers of deception'.[74] When exchange ceased or where it was conducted on the basis of labour time, the primary cause of economic immorality had been removed. Where abundance prevailed ill-will and individual antagonism had no material basis. Where each contributed according to ability and received according to need, economic life would be established on unshakeable moral foundations.

Clearly, then, communitarian socialism did furnish a political economy for the working class. Yet there were, in the 1830s and 1840s, alternative visions of the material basis on which a socialist society might rest. There were other views as to how and with what objectives a socialist economy might be constituted – views that were, ultimately, to prove more appealing to the working class. It is with these that the remaining chapters of this book will be concerned.

CHAPTER 7

The *Pioneer*, 1833–34 and the Political Economy of Syndicalism

The late 1820s and early 1830s in Britain were a period of economic depression characterised by falling prices, glutted markets, general unemployment and, therefore, an intensification of competitive pressures in the markets for both labour and goods. What this entailed, among other things, was an acceleration in some of those developments noted in Chapter 3. The expansion of sweating, subcontracting and deskilling proceeded apace in trades such as tailoring, shoemaking, building and carpentry; artisan masters 'sank' into the ranks of the sweated or 'rose' to become small masters and sweating exploiters in their own right. By subcontracting, the extension of short-term credit, discounting the prices of small-scale suppliers through the exercise of monopsony power and by means of other expedients, larger firms exerted greater control over their smaller counterparts, so forcing them to adopt a more exploitative attitude to their workforce.[1] Specifically this meant in many trades the substitution of piece rates for day rates, the diminution of the piece rates already established, the erosion of customary notions of what length and amount of work might properly be expected, and what expedients, such as work-sharing, might legitimately be entertained when times were bad.

It was against such a fraught economic backdrop too that those working-class aspirations which had been raised by the campaign for, and prospect of, a substantial measure of political reform were dashed by the passage of a Reform Act which, whatever else it did, left an overwhelming majority of the population disenfranchised. For many of those who had been engaged in the agitation for reform, this was seen as a great betrayal of their best hopes and endeavours; it was seen too as one perpetrated by the middle classes. It was they who had engaged working-class energies, canalising them into Political Unions which applied pressure on Parliament, both by their radical demands and through the implied threat of the social upheaval that might ensue should those demands be refused. Many, therefore, saw themselves as having been used as a cat's paw by means of which the middle class had secured for itself, from the landed interest, a measure of political power to complement that growing economic strength which, particularly in time of depression, it deployed to coercive and exploitative effect.

It is in this context that the unprecedented levels of working-class agitation and activity that characterised the 1830s can best be set – the rapid growth of support for co-operation, the sudden burgeoning of labour exchanges, the proliferation of a vibrantly assertive working-class press and, above all, the explosion of trade union activity in varied and novel forms. Some of these developments have already been noted, but what is different in the early 1830s is their scale, the manner in which they become interwoven and the ideological, organisational and social consequences which this had. Thus, as regards trade unionism, there was the emergence of national and general unions such as the cotton textile workers' National Association for the Protection of Labour, the Operative Builders' Union, the Potters' Union, the Grand Lodge of Operative Tailors in London and the Grand National Consolidated Trades' Union of 1834, in whose formation the tailors, saddlemakers and cabinet makers played a crucial role.[2] Of course intra- and inter-trade co-operation by means of unions was not new. But it had never taken place on the scale (geographically or in terms of numbers), nor with the organisational sophistication and the degree of working-class support which it mustered in the early 1830s. What Sykes has written of the National Association for the Protection of Labour is more generally true of trade unionism in this period. 'The NAPL, simply as a general union, was not unprecedented, but in size, geographical extent, duration, sophistication, ambitions and class outlook, it did represent much that was new. It was not merely a stage in an unchanging tradition of inter-trade co-operation.'[3] Or, as Postgate wrote of the builders,

> whatever beginnings of national organisation may have been made, they were insignificant until the great union took them over in 1832. In that year the Operative Builders' Union ... comes into prominence, and by its activities turns small feeble societies into one national body, powerful in its own great membership and careful organisation.[4]

Further, as never before, such activity was informed and inspired by a co-operative political economy disseminated by a working-class press which, through papers such as the *Pioneer*, the *Crisis*, the *Voice of the People*, the *Voice of the West Riding* and the *Herald to the Rights of Industry*, gave support and offered guidance to the general and national unions which had emerged. Trade unionism became infused with co-operative ideas and sought to translate these ideas into practice. Trade societies in London had co-operated to establish the United Trades' Association which organised co-operative production to service the equitable labour exchanges. The idea of co-operative production was also to acquire a particular significance in the wave of industrial conflict which characterised the period 1833–34. The silk weavers in Derby, the tailors in London, the builders in Birmingham and in other towns, the shoemakers of Northamptonshire, and else-where, organised co-operative production both to support those who had taken strike action and to employ those whom depres-sion had rendered redundant. Of course it must be said that, like inter-union co-operation, such expedients were not peculiar to the 1830s. They had been adopted before to enhance bargaining power and beat employers. But the extent of these activities, their integration with the idea of labour exchanges and labour banks, the scale on which they were undertaken and, as we shall see, the manner in which they were interwoven with a vision of an autonomous workers' economy, where employers and owners of capital had become superfluous, does render them qualitatively different from what had gone before.

Much of the industrial conflict in the period was also charac-terised by the expression of an acute sense of class antagonism. In the aftermath of 1832 such antagonism had political roots and found expression in the radical political discourse of organisations such as the National Union of the Working Classes. But it was also enunciated in the language and categories of political economy. Indeed in Bronterre O'Brien, editor of the *Poor Man's Guardian*, we have a fusion, often an uneasy one, of the discourses of political radicalism *and* anti-capitalist political economy. Thus it was not just the 'taxeater' but also the 'profitmongers' who loomed large in the demonology that O'Brien constructed. For other writers in the working-class press, however, the language was more purely that of political economy and the economic roots of class antagonism more clearly identified – 'War, war, war, labour declares war against capital', proclaimed a headline in the *Pioneer*, a rallying call echoed and re-echoed by other elements of the working-class press.

It was clear too that many employers viewed industrial conflict and the rapid growth of trade unionism in a markedly similar light to that of the *Pioneer*. Employers' combinations had a long history and were not merely a response to this upsurge of trade union activity. However, their militancy in the early 1830s can certainly be understood in that context. To give just a few examples. In Northamptonshire employers agreed not to employ members of the shoemakers' union, with anyone departing from this injunc-tion made liable to a forfeiture of £40.[5] 1833 saw schemes for a masters' union in the building trade to destroy the Builders' Union; an objective duly accomplished by the autumn of 1834. In the Derby silk weaving industry, in the building trade and in others, employers insisted that employees sign 'The Document' renouncing their trade union membership. More generally employers had recourse to lockouts, arrests of union members and officials, victimisation and legal action of the kind that, in 1834, saw the transportation of the Tolpuddle martyrs. So the sense of political betrayal was now compounded by the antagonism felt for those who used both judicial and material power to crush the destitute and vulnerable in a period of depression. This antagonism was further intensified when, in 1834, the 'reformed' Parliament passed the Poor Law Amendment Act, which instituted a less eligibility principle to govern the level of poor relief and insisted on its future dispensation through the medium of the workhouse.

In such circumstances and, in particular, with the aid of a working-class press, socialist political economy was always likely to extend its influence and, as we shall see, take new and more radical forms. That said, of course, one must be careful not to exaggerate its influence on working-class organisations and activity in the period. Glen, in a study of Stockport, found that 'trade unions ... generally sought limited objectives and rarely developed critiques of the capitalist system'. Sykes in his discussion of the NAPL has emphasised the 'patchy and limited' influence of Owenism and stressed that the NAPL was never an Owenite union.[6] Prothero's discussion of the tailors' strike, in the spring of 1834, has emphasised the traditional nature of the demands they advanced:

> all work must be done on proper employers' premises ... hours must be limited so as to share work; piece work which led to overwork must be ended; the day-rate must be fixed ... A proper amount of work would be guaranteed by the traditional daily stint.[7]

Such objectives were clearly inspired by the notions of a moral economy and it is certainly the case too that co-operative production and labour exchanges were strongly supported by artisans whose primary objective was the recovery of their traditional status and independence.[8] Similarly, Postgate stressed that 'the building trade workers were in reality looking backwards, the basis of their revolutionary feeling was anger at the loss of past good conditions'.[9]

However, as Fryson has shown, it is clear that Owenite socialism was influential within the Potters' Union, inspiring plans for co-

operative stores and a Potters' Labour Bank.[10] In addition, while
the NAPL was 'never an Owenite union', 'two important textile
unions, the dyers and calico printers, did forge links with local
Owenites when they established their own major co-operative
production schemes in 1830–33'.[11] Also, as regards the Tailors'
Union, many of its leaders had been involved with the producers'
co-operatives which had constituted the London United Trades'
Association and two tailors' co-operative societies had supplied the
National Equitable Labour Exchange.[12] It was also the case that
Robert Owen's involvement with trade unionism in the early 1830s
period and, in particular, the Grand National Consolidated
Trades' Union, also acted as a means of disseminating the
economic philosophy of co-operative socialism. Of much greater
general importance here, though, was the working-class press.

Yet, whatever the impact of socialist political economy on the
organisations and activity of the working class, it is clear that the
events of the early 1830s also left their mark on the socialist
economic thinking of the period. Specifically, the formation of
national and general unions using co-operative production, labour
exchanges and labour banks, led writers such as J.F. Bray, James
Morrison, the editor of the *Pioneer*, and J.E. 'Shepherd' Smith, the
editor of the Owenite socialist paper, the *Crisis*,[13] to theorise the
possibility of a parallel socialist economy operating independently
of, but ultimately engulfing, existing economic arrangements. As
we shall see in this and the next chapter, these writers were to give
the artisan aspiration for independence a decidedly collectivist
dimension, predicating it upon the social ownership of the means
of production and, through labour exchanges and labour notes, the
socialisation of the means of distribution and exchange.

One might suggest too that the intensity and nature of the industrial conflict which distinguished the early 1830s also drove home
with unparalleled force the contemporary nature and locus of
economic power. Lockouts and 'The Document', showed that the
power to exploit and impoverish derived from ownership of the
means of production and thence the capacity to deny access to the
means of labour and livelihood. Strikes were broken by the capitalist through the use of such power. Further, as noted in Chapter
3, the early nineteenth century did see, however slow the process,
a gradual increase in the scale of those means and, therefore, the
economic strength derived from that source. Thus this period was
characterised by the extension of mechanisation, by a growth in the
scale of productive enterprise and, for the economy as a whole, an
increase in the importance of fixed capital investment.[14]

Taken together, these developments pointed in one direction. If
labour was to secure its whole product, if an economy was to be
constructed where the principles of economic equity prevailed, if

the continued expansion and full utilisation of the nation's formidable and growing productive capacity were to occur and periods of
depression and impoverishment avoided and, crucially, if the
exploitative and coercive power of capitalist employers was to be
broken, then the existing means of production must pass, by
whatever expedient, from private, grasping hands into social
ownership.

As we shall see in Chapter 8, this idea was to be taken up and
elaborated in the political economy of John Gray and John Francis
Bray, writers who considered that the ownership of the means of
production, distribution and exchange should be vested in the
nation as a whole. However, it was also to be developed by James
Morrison, J.E. Smith and others in the trade union paper the
Pioneer, though in a very different and essentially neo-syndicalist
fashion and it is with that paper, these writers and their distinctive
socialist political economy that this chapter will be concerned.

The *Pioneer* or, to give it its full title, the *Pioneer or Grand
National Consolidated Trades' Union Magazine*, first appeared on 7
September 1833 and the last issue was published on the 5 July
1834. It was edited by James Morrison and, as its long title
suggests, it concerned itself primarily with the activities of trade
unions and the general labour unrest which characterised the
period 1833–34. It has been described as 'one of the best-known
trades union and co-operative miscellanies of the decade'.[15] At its
peak, its circulation was probably around the 20,000. Few papers
other than the *Poor Man's Guardian* attained such popularity in
this period. In looking at the political economy it purveyed, this
chapter will be primarily concerned with the editorials of James
Morrison and a series of letters, the *Letters on Associated Labour*,
published under the pseudonym 'Senex' and variously attributed
to Morrison or the editor of the *Crisis*, J.E. Smith.[16] However, the
contributions of some other, usually pseudonymous, correspon-
dents will also be considered.

The explanation of working-class impoverishment to be most
frequently found in the *Pioneer* is recognisably that advanced in
the work of writers such as Hodgskin, Thompson, Gray and, later
in the 1830s, J.F. Bray. Labour was seen as the sole source of
value. Capital, both fixed and circulating, was necessary for
production, but that too was clearly furnished by labour.

> We know that the operative manufacturer, and, in fact, the
> labourer of every description, requires sustenance, raw mat-
> erials and tools. *These are derived from the reserved produce of
> former labour, which is termed capital.* The amount of capital in
> this country is very great; but, brethren, it was you that gave it
> existence.[17]

However, while labour gave existence to capital, its ownership resided with others and was used by them to determine labour's material condition. Thus, the owners of capital had transmuted workers into 'hireling labour', 'selling their lives, piecemeal, by the day, the week, the month or the year', purchasing only 'so much of a man as they [the capitalists] can make any profit of'.[18] It was the power of capital to commoditise labour that was at the root of labour's impoverishment and the corresponding enrichment of the capitalist.

Such a perception of the source of economic power, and the consequences of its location in hands other than those of the working class, led on to the view that those who sought to improve the condition and status of labour by purely political means were dissipating their energies on matters of little moment. As Senex stated:

> as I looked at the condition of my fellow beings; as I looked closely into the state of dependence in which myself, and men dependent like me, for their daily bread on the sale they can obtain for their weekly labour in a market of which the profit-mongering capitalists have the control, and of which their House of Commons is the market-clerk, I have paused and exclaimed ... social liberty must precede political liberty.[19]

Such was the subordinate status of Parliament, such the nature of its association with the possessors of economic power, reflecting the more general relationship which was seen as existing between the political and the economic. The former was subservient to the latter. It was the possession of the means of production, not formal political rights which conferred real authority. Any substantial improvement in the condition of the working class must take that as its starting point. Social must precede political liberty.

Thus 'revolutions' such as those of 1688 and 1789 did not advance in the least

> the real interests of the labouring classes, in either France or England; and were one of these government revolutions to take place at the present period ... the producers would not ... be benefited by it ... whether this party holds the helm of power, or that party with large promises of attention to the interests of the people, endeavours by our assistance to seize upon the management of the same helm, we must continue as we were before – the ill-paid servants, the hard-working slaves of the consuming and non-productive classes of the state.

This was so because 'state power' was 'so blind and infatuated – so much the tool of the interests of a mere handful of capitalists', that little could be expected even from a thoroughly reformed parliament.[20] 'Would prosperity and justice be attained, even if our legislature should at once be constituted to combine all the leading liberals of the day, freed from all legal authority?' asked one writer, answering that 'the working classes' should not

> delude themselves by anticipating the least benefit from such changes: let them be assured that, so long as the government is a servile instrument of a rich and idle aristocracy, the interests of the people will be sacrificed to the aggrandizement of these rapacious despoilers; and however talented, however honest, however uncompromising our legislators may be ... they will irresistibly be urged to the adoption of measures similar to those which have hitherto enslaved and depressed the workmen.[21]

To widen the franchise, to eliminate rotten boroughs, to dispense with placemen and pensioners was to indulge in the futile exercise of 'reforming the more decorative parts of society, whilst the foundation is suffered to remain unsound and rotten'.[22]

That foundation was economic and its rottenness derived from the poverty-stricken condition of labour. 'True radical reform' therefore involved tackling that problem. 'Instead of cobbling up the system of government, let us re-model that from which all government proceeds, and for which it exists – our own working condition. This will be the true radical reform – beginning with the root and extending through the trunk to the extreme branches.'[23] Here, just as radical political reform was rejected as ineffectual, so was the economic reform programme to which political radicals had subscribed.

> Their eyes are so short-sighted that they look only to partial release – the diminution of taxation, the separation of church and state, the revision of the pension-list, and such other milk-and-water favours; and when they have received these boons, pray where are they? Is the power of private capital and monopoly in any wise impaired? Is the system of commercial competition paralysed?[24]

These were the crucial economic criteria by reference to which the efficacy or otherwise of any reform programme must be judged: the extent to which it eroded the economic power wielded by capitalists and how far it supplanted the existing system of commercial competition. By such standards political radicalism was clearly ineffectual.

Along with this elucidation of the economic power of the capitalist class as both emasculating political radicalism and impoverishing labour went the articulation of a growing sense of class identity and class antagonism. As to the former, 'it is certain', stated one writer, 'that as knowledge extends, the habit of thinking and of acting with the majority of the class to which we belong, extends also in a still greater ratio ... As intelligence spreads this feeling of the necessity of men who have the same interests acting with one mind, spreads also.'[25] Such was certainly true of contemporary 'workingmen' who 'will support each other to the last hour of their lives', for '*they have only one interest to protect*'.[26] Those constituting other classes could not be trusted. Labourers must rely on their own efforts and those of their own class for any improvement of their position. 'Did any of you ever know a rich man speak of you respectfully? Did any of you ever hear a man of power applaud a single virtue you possess ... ? In any struggle who befriends us? In any danger who protects? In any ignominy who pities us? Trust none who is a grade above our class ... Trust none of them.'[27] Thus did the editor of the *Pioneer* exhort his readership, while holding out the prospect of the social and material emancipation which such solidarity was already effecting. 'Your class', wrote the editor of the *Pioneer*, 'is the first which has arisen in the majesty of its strength to assert its own independence'.[28]

A concomitant notion of an intensifying class struggle was also forcefully expressed. 'The capitalist is continually accumulating, and the working man continually going down; and this will continue to operate, until the injured labourer, galled by intolerable oppression, shall rise with a determination which nothing can quell, and effect a dreadful revolution.' Meanwhile, on the other side of a widening social divide, 'masters' were organising 'to crush the spirit of our class'.[29] The gulf was unbridgeable and the interests of capital and labour irreconcilable. 'The struggle between profits and wages' could not 'cease until wages are completely victorious, or the manufactory is to the productive labourers the same thing as the workhouse'.[30]

One sees as well in the *Pioneer* what one finds in Hodgskin's *Labour Defended*, namely an attempt to differentiate the legitimate reward accruing to 'masters' for their labour of superintendence and direction, from gains derived from the exploitative use of the power which capital conferred upon them. Such a distinction allowed writers to argue that the interests of masters and men were the same, while simultaneously writing of the increasing antagonism between them. In so far as the recompense of masters derived solely from the superior labour which they performed, then, indeed, there was a harmony of interests. 'Directors and guides must always exist' and they should be rewarded. But

where, as was increasingly the case, it was the intent of masters 'to
get ... labour as cheap as possible ... to use machinery to supersede it' and to reduce 'the real producer of wealth' to a point
where he 'scarcely obtains for his labour the necessaries of life',
then their interests were antagonistic to those of the labouring
class.[31] In effect, what writers argued was that to the extent that
masters secured their income through the use of fixed and circulating capital, they ceased to be labourers. Social conflict with
those who did was then inevitable. But, as a result of some of the
economic developments noted above, that is exactly what many
masters were increasingly doing.

It was hoped that a time would come when

> he who guides by his superior intellect shall not, as now, direct
> and govern for his own individual advantage; nor shall the
> power that is conferred upon the superintendent of a branch of
> trade be the selfish power of a monopolist, but the social power
> of a servant of the public. He that is the greatest amongst the
> people shall be the servant of all.[32]

Yet, that would only be the case when a different set of socio-
economic arrangements prevailed; when labour, through its
unions, came to own and control the nation's productive
capacity. To remedy labour's economic impotence it was vital
that it secured access to the sources of power. To this end trade
unionists were exhorted

> to devise the means of founding manufactories, cultivating
> land, building ships, establishing trades, opening communica-
> tions from the Unionists of one part of the kingdom with
> another, and transacting business by exchanging produce for
> produce, on our own account with the industrious and skilful
> people of other countries.

The author of the *Letters* wrote similarly of the need for 'large
partnership manufactories' trading between themselves.[33] The
vision is an essentially syndicalist one of a decentralised socialism
in which trades unions or groups of trade unionists have acquired,
by whatever means, the productive capacity to render themselves
collectively self-sufficient as a class. It is also, in contrast to
communitarian socialism, a vision which encompassed the idea of
industry, commerce and even international trade. As such it is
more obviously in harmony with an industrialising Britain, even if
there is, in the *Pioneer*, a continuing emphasis on the need to
acquire land in order to provide the most basic means of subsistence. However, even where trade unionists were encouraged to

'get land [and] withdraw yourselves from large towns' it was in order that they should become 'manufacturing colonists'.[34] As to the means by which the productive capacity would be acquired, the primary view seems to have been that once trade unionists, even on a small scale, began exchanging amongst themselves, then the profits which had previously accumulated in the hands of the capitalist would accrue to the unions and this would furnish the necessary investment funds.

So the advantages of a social division of labour are recognised, as too are the benefits to be derived from domestic commerce and international trade. To secure these it was necessary not only that 'combinations' be 'formed amongst them [trade unionists] to produce for themselves and each other', but also '*modes of exchange arranged*, to prevent the possibility of the capitalist cheating them out of the fruits of their toil'. To this end it would be requisite to 'establish a bank and a circulating medium', which would ensure that labour exchanged against labour and exploitative unequal exchanges ceased.[35] Thus

> the labourers of the country who create everything, ought also to create the money, and then they could always have a sufficient quantity to give them a free exchange of labour ... If the productive classes would make their own paper money to represent the value of the various kinds of wealth actually made, and to enable them without difficulty to exchange one sort for another, they would raise their condition in six months, to a higher state of comfort and prosperity than was ever before experienced in the world.[36]

In effect, a socialised banking system would play a vital role in integrating the different collectivities which constituted this syndicalist economy.

As regards the reward of the labour which constituted these 'partnership manufactories', 'manufacturing colonies' or collectively organised 'trades', this would be determined on the basis of certain agreed principles. One writer proposed 'a grand COURT OF ARBITRATION to establish the price and value of labour of every kind'. The editor wrote of such 'a well-organised body of tradesmen, guided by laws of their own enactment; creating wealth for their mutual benefit and *distributing that wealth in just proportions to each member of the fraternity*'. 'Such an organisation' collectively ordering both the production and equitable distribution of wealth was seen by the writer 'as near approaching perfection as we can make. It is the ultimatum of the progress of society; the beau ideal which we ought at all times to have transfigured [*sic*] before us; a stimulant to exertion, and a compass to direct our movements.'[37] However, whatever mechanism was used to establish a just remuneration for labour, the crucial point was that that reward would no longer be determined in a market in which the economic dice were loaded heavily in favour of its capitalist buyer. Labour would cease to be a marketable commodity subject to the vagaries of market forces – or worse, a prey to the avaricious instincts of those who collusively or individually could manipulate those forces to their advantage.

> Do you ask me how you are to alter your condition ... how you are to prevent your labour from being thus marketable to the lowest bidder? I tell you fearlessly and confidently, that if you will unite in one common body – one common union – you will soon discover the means are at hand ... to remedy the evils which afflict you and afflict society generally.[38]

For the author of the *Letters* the aim was to 'banish the word wages from the language and consign it, with the word slavery to histories and dictionaries. Wages is a term of purchase; it means the piece-meal purchase of your blood, and bones, and brains at weekly payments.'[39]

Such goals could be achieved independently of radical political reform but their attainment would, at the same time, involve the construction of a new polity which would ultimately render the old redundant. Here writers like Senex drew out some of the political implications of the syndicalism to which they adhered. Society and government would be reconstructed by means of this radical redistribution of the source of economic power; an alteration in the material base would, ultimately, transfigure the political and social superstructure. 'We have determined', wrote the editor of the *Pioneer*,

> that REFORM shall commence from within. We govern within ourselves, and conceive it to be a duty to acquaint ourselves of the principles of government, consisting simply in good internal regulations. We feel that to regulate trade, or the several branches of labour by which we live, will most speedily regulate government. These are the means we should adopt for the end and we hold them to be more powerful than petitioning. We know that universal suffrage may be obtained by these means.[40]

There are three propositions here with a bearing on the nature of the polity which was expected to emerge from the decentralised socialism which the *Pioneer* advanced. The first is that working-class ownership and management of the means of production would instil a capacity for democratic government in those who participated in producing unions and 'manufacturing partnerships'. The second is that the acquisition and use of the power necessary to regulate economic activity would, in effect, ensure the control of government. The third is that the working-class control of economic power would be the means by which, directly or indirectly, universal suffrage could be secured.

The idea that union ownership and control of productive capacity would render existing political authority impotent and allow the working class to create a different institutional structure for its exercise of *de facto* political power was also developed elsewhere in the *Pioneer*. As the editor put it, with respect to what he saw as the growing economic power of the Grand National Consolidated Trades' Union,

> we are thoroughly convinced that, when it is sufficiently organised ... it will gradually draw into its vortex all the commercial interest of the country, and, in so doing, it will become, by its own self-acquired importance, a most influential, we might almost say dictatorial, part of the body politic. When this happens ... we have gained universal suffrage; for if every member of the Union be a constituent, and the Union itself become a vital and influential member of the state, it instantly erects itself into a House of Trades, which must supply the place of the present House of Commons, and direct the commercial affairs of the country, according to the will of the trades who compose the associations of industry.[41]

Others were to argue in a similar fashion. 'See sir into what position this mode of pursuing things resolves itself. Every trade has its internal government in every town; a certain number of towns comprise a district, and delegates from the trades in each town form a quarterly district government; delegates from the districts form an Annual Parliament; and the King of England becomes President of the Trades' Unions!'[42] Thus the General Union, comprising as it would a multiplicity of unions each of which would regulate the economic affairs of the trade, industry or sector of industry over which it had secured control, would ultimately constitute a House of Trades or true House of Commons to replace that which served not the commons but the interests of the capitalist and landowning classes.[43] As one anonymous writer put it, in this way, having won economic power and rendered the aristocracy impotent, labourers would

> secure their freedom from political slavery, and establish a government, which shall supersede all the vacillating, profit-

making, unprincipled legislatures, which have heretofore
enriched the idle few, and bound in blind ignorance and destitute misery the industrious many.[44]

In such a context the existing House of Commons would either
wither away or, in so far as it was deemed to have a role with
respect, for example, to foreign affairs, it would be allowed to
fulfil it only on the understanding that it would 'govern well and
wisely, according to the new light which ... trade unions will
develop upon the subject'.[45]

These were to be the salient characteristics of the polity which
might be expected to arise from the material basis of the kind of
syndicalism which the *Pioneer* propagated. Here again, therefore,
we have a political economy for the working class which clearly
transcended the limitations of political radicalism both in terms of
its conceptual sophistication, its critical analysis and its prescriptive intent.

What the *Pioneer* advanced was a decentralised conception of a
socialist economy where ownership of productive capacity came
to reside in the hands of co-operative enterprises and trades'
unions, with the latter exerting a measure of co-ordination and
control over particular sectors of economic activity. But, in the
1830s, others also elaborated a conception of a socialist economy
predicated upon the social ownership of the means of production.
In contrast, though, it was one which emphasised the centralisation of such ownership in the nation and, along with that, stressed
the need for the central co-ordination and control of economic
activity. Such writers advanced, in effect, a political economy of
state socialism with planning authorities supplanting the market
and undertaking the pricing, distributive, allocative and equilibrating functions which it was deemed by classical writers to
perform. It is the salient elements of such a socialist political
economy as it was formulated by two writers, John Gray and John
Francis Bray, which will be considered in the next chapter.

CHAPTER 8

The Political Economy of Socialist Planning: John Gray and John Francis Bray

John Gray (*c*.1799–1883) was born around the turn of the century, educated, between the ages of nine and 13 at Repton School, Derbyshire and then, at the age of 14, employed in a manufacturing and wholesale house in Cheapside. It was from this time on, he informs us, that he concerned himself with the reform of the social system.[1] This inspired him to write what proved to be an abortive tract on social reform entitled *The National Commercial System* and then, at the instigation of his brother, to take an interest in the ideas of Robert Owen, whom he heard speak at a series of debates on co-operation which took place at the London Tavern in 1817. It was, however, some years before Gray once again committed his ideas to paper. His first published work, *A Lecture on Human Happiness*, was published in January 1825.

Gray claimed that he had arrived at the central ideas of this book independently of Owen, but it is a work which certainly reflected many of the central concerns of Owenite socialism. It was, in essence, an indictment of competitive capitalism which, in Gray's view, had produced a distribution of wealth skewed in favour of the unproductive part of the nation and detrimental to those whose labour was its source.[2] This maldistribution was effected primarily by means of unequal exchanges. It was 'exclusively by barter, that the power, by which individuals are enabled to tyrannize over nations, is introduced into the world'.[3] Such exchanges 'depriv[ing]' the 'productive classes' 'of very nearly four fifths of the produce of their labour'.[4]

In impoverishing labour in this manner the competitive system also created a demand constraint upon the full utilisation of productive capacity, labour included.[5] 'Thus competition limits the quantity of wealth obtained by individuals: the quantity obtained by individuals collectively composes the aggregate quantity obtained by the whole community: this aggregate quantity forms the demand, and demand limits production.'[6] In a way characteristic of early nineteenth-century socialist political

economy, Gray therefore linked the twin evils of labour exploitation and general economic depression.

These were to be the central themes taken up and elaborated
more fully in *The Social System, a Treatise on the Principle of
Exchange*, 1831, in which the critical analysis proceeded along
very similar lines to the *Lecture*. However, while in the *Lecture*
Gray was to see the evils which he identified as being eliminated
through the formation of co-operative communities,[7] within
which competitive exchanges would not occur, in *The Social
System* Gray headed, prescriptively, in a very different direction.

For the Gray of *The Social System*, as of the *Lecture*, it was 'our
system of exchange which forms the hiding place of that giant of
mischief which bestrides the civilized world, rewarding industry
with starvation, exertion with disappointment, and the best efforts
of our rulers to do good, with perplexity, dismay and failure'.[8]
Thus it was in the context of the existing system of exchange that
labour was exploited. 'No system of commerce', he wrote,

> can be conceived more monstrously at variance with the equi-
> table principle ... than that which compels the poor man to
> sell his labour by public competition. He might as well sell
> himself; nay, according to some accounts, it would be much
> better for him to sell his person, than to sell, in the manner he
> does at present, the labour of his hands. We have a nominal
> system of commercial freedom, but a real system of commer-
> cial slavery.[9]

Also, as in the *Lecture*, so in the *Social System*, a link is made
between the defective system of exchange and the deficient
demand which precipitated glutted markets, underutilised
productive capacity and a wholesale redundancy of labour.

However, while the connection between labour exploitation
and general depression is certainly there, in *The Social System*
emphasis is shifted in that work to the disequilibrating role played
by the existing medium of exchange. Specifically what Gray
discussed at length in the 1831 work was the failure of the money
supply, under competitive capitalism, to expand *pari passu* with
the growth of output. The problem was that 'money' failed to
'increase as produce ... increased' or 'decrease as produce [was]
... consumed'. Deficient monetary demand and glutted markets
were the inevitable consequence. 'Gluts of one thing, we are told,
merely argue a corresponding deficiency of some other thing; but
unless that other thing be money it is an evident absurdity to
attribute them to any such cause.'[10] It was the consequent difficulties which entrepreneurs had in selling their wares at a
profitable price in markets glutted for want of a sufficient money

demand which led them to reduce output and lay off labour. With glutted markets there arose

> a powerful check upon production; the fear of producing too much; the fear lest the article should fetch less money than it cost ... Great care must be taken that goods be not made so freely, as to lower themselves in money price, because the undertaker would, in that case lose by his adventure, his object being to gain by it.[11]

Contrary to the view of the classical economists, therefore, there was, under existing commercial arrangements, no mechanism equilibrating supply and demand at a macroeconomic level. On the contrary, there were powerful forces making for general economic depression. A deficient demand resulting from a defective medium of exchange combined with a competitive system of unequal exchanges to act as a powerful and constantly operating check on the expansion of output and the realisation of that potential for abundance which mechanisation had created.

These, clearly, were interconnected problems which could not be solved by the kind of political reforms for which radicals pressed. On the inefficacy of political remedies, the *Lecture* and *The Social System* are again consistent. 'Give us', wrote Gray,

> parliamentary reform, give us universal suffrage, annual parliaments, vote by ballot, an acquittal of the public debt, freedom from all taxes, a repeal of the Union, and every other thing upon which the public has ever yet rested its disappointed hopes – and still shall this demon of commercial error hold our prosperity in his iron grasp, and smile upon our ignorance and folly as he shall see our burdens ... one by one removed, whilst we continue to sink deeper and deeper still into the Slough of Despond, under the invisible but enormous weight that is oppressing us.[12]

For Gray, therefore, it was

> totally impossible, by any means that the ingenuity of man can contrive, ever to govern this, or any country, in such a manner as to ensure the general prosperity of its people, until the existing plan of exchange be uprooted from society, and another substituted for it, by which production would be rendered the constant cause of demand.[13]

So in place of the existing flawed system of competitive exchange operating on the basis of a medium which continually failed to

keep pace with the growth of output, and in place of the irra-
tionality, uncertainty, waste, self-seeking, exploitative behaviour
and consequent social antagonism which characterised a competitive order prone to macroeconomic depression, Gray proposed
the purposive planning and direction of economic activity as the
foundation for a new 'social' system of exchange. It was this that
would furnish the basis for economic equity, economic progress,
abundance and social harmony.

This idea of planning is touched on in his *Lecture*, but in the
Social System it occupied a more central place in his political
economy.[14] In both works the putative self-ordering and equilibrating properties of the competitive market were discounted.

> A notion appears to prevail amongst mankind, that there exists
> in our Social System a self-regulating principle, and that the
> stream of commerce like that of water, only requires to be let
> alone to find its own level, and to flow on smoothly and pros-
> perously. Ten years ago, I doubted, and I now deny, the
> existence of any such principle.[15]

The depressed state of the contemporary economy manifestly
illustrated the absence of any self-regulating mechanisms and
highlighted the need for 'a thoroughly organized plan of production, exchange, distribution, and accumulation'.[16] Here Gray
contrasted the contemporary micro-and the macro-economy. At
a microeconomic level production was increasingly characterised
by conscious planning, organisation and control. There was,
however, no replication of this at a macroeconomic level. Thus,

> whilst contrivance, arrangement, plan, are indispensably
> necessary to every part, the aggregate of parts is left to work, as
> best it can, ungoverned: and thus, whilst God requires arrange-
> ment and a plan to govern worlds, presumptuous man sets at
> defiance his makers laws, and tells the paltry objects of his care
> to rule themselves.[17]

So what was to be the institutional basis for such economic
planning? By whom and by what means would planning be implemented? On what principles and with what objectives would it
proceed? Taking the second question first. Gray is clear that the
power to plan was derived from the ownership of the means of
production. The power to plan nationally would therefore require
the collective ownership of those means. The passage from
private to collective ownership would occur voluntarily with
owners of capital and land who recognised the necessity and
utility of planning coming together to establish an association. By

way of compensation they would have 'an estimated value put on' what they had previously owned and then 'receive a fixed annual remuneration for the use thereof, proportionate to its value, in lieu of retaining in their own hands, the chance of gain or loss by its cultivation or employment'.[18] So a voluntary surrender of assets would be compensated for by the equivalent of a national annuity yielding a fixed income stream. Ultimately the aim should be to create 'a national capital, consisting of land, mines, manufactories, warehouses, shipping, machinery, implements, and, in short, of every thing required in the production, exchange and distribution of commodities';[19] or, in more modern parlance, the ultimate objective was the nationalisation of the means of production, distribution and exchange.

Gray fully expected the existing owners of productive capacity to acquiesce in all this. His proposals offered them the certainty of a fixed income stream as against the angst, the risk, the uncertainty and the volatility which existing economic arrangements inflicted upon them. 'Let them', wrote Gray,

> think deeply upon the principle of exchange that is here explained, and let each ask himself as an individual, whether he would not prefer becoming an agent to the British nation, responsible only to an elected power for his proceedings, on receiving a fixed, a certain and a liberal remuneration for the performance of a plain, an easy, and an honourable duty, to remaining the never-ending slave of caprice, uncertainty, incessant toil, and interminable anxiety.[20]

Having reflected thus there could be only one conclusion. Once collective ownership had been established those whose land and capital had been consolidated in this way would elect a National Chamber of Commerce which would be the key institution as regards the formulation and implementation of the economic plan. This would comprise 'a president, and a sufficient number of representatives, [to] be chosen in an equitable manner'.[21] However, while Gray alludes to the equitable manner of their choice, he clearly envisaged that these 'representatives' would be drawn from those who already wielded economic authority and had experience of the organisation and direction of economic activity. The National Chamber could, after all, only be elected from those who had, originally, been possessed of 'land, buildings, machinery, goods or money',[22] it must come from those who had originally acquiesced in the collectivisation of their productive resources. Gray's solution to the problem of economic leadership in a planned economy was, therefore, decidedly meritocratic and technocratic rather than democratic.

In this National Chamber of Commerce would be vested the 'supreme (economic) power' necessary to direct and control 'all cultivation, manufactures, and trade'.[23] Further 'every distinct branch of trade, commerce, and manufactures, would [come] ... to be conducted by a committee of men, (members of the Chamber of Commerce) thoroughly and practically acquainted with it', as also would 'the direction of foreign commerce, both as respects exportation and importation'.[24] Here again we have a technocratic emphasis, Gray's expectation being that it would be existing 'proprietors of capital possessing also the *requisite knowledge*' of production who 'should in all convenient cases be appointed' agents of the National Chamber.[25]

Gray clearly anticipated that the existing owners of productive capacity would be the primary agency by means of which his proposals would be implemented. However, he also argued that the 'labouring classes' themselves might seize the initiative. 'It is certain', Gray declared

> from their overwhelming numbers, that they could, of themselves, and without any assistance whatever, put the principles of the Social System into operation. For, in every state of society, the wages of labour must be sufficient to support the toils of labour ... and this minimum reward or 'natural price of labour', as the political economists call it, can never be so nicely adjusted, but that the labouring classes may be enabled to save something out of their earnings; and, though a farthing a week should be fixed as a minimum subscription, it is certain that, for a great national object, such as is here contended for, so complete a system of voluntary tax might be established ... as speedily to realize a sum sufficient to start the Social System; and, once fairly on its legs, it would be easier to retard the tides than check its progress.[26]

Here Gray seems to move closer to those communitarian socialists who saw in the savings of the working classes the means by which the foundation of the new order might be laid. Yet the aim is not the formation of autarchic co-operative communities. The objective is the collective ownership of means of production sufficient to lay the basis for national economic planning. Further, it is only through the accumulation and possession of capital that the working class can create and participate in the kind of socialist economy that Gray has in mind.

Once established on the basis of an adequate 'national capital', the National Chamber of commerce would consciously determine all those matters that had previously been the unplanned outcome of market forces.

It will be already understood, that the Social System recognises as useful, but one controlling and directing power, but one judge of what it is prudent and proper to bring into the market, either as respects kind or quantity, – the Chamber of Commerce, – who, having the means of ascertaining, at all times, the actual stock of any kind of goods on hand, would always be able to say at once where production should proceed more rapidly, where at its usual pace, and where also it should be retarded.[27]

As regards the latter, Gray was adamant that the National Chamber would shut down productive capacity and allocate the resources released to the production of those goods and services the demand for which remained unsatisfied. So,

> whenever any commodity shall be found to be unduly accumulating in the national warehouses, thereby proving that it is unnecessary to continue its production, to the same extent as formerly, a portion of the capital and labour employed in the production of the said article, [will] be forthwith devoted to another purpose.[28]

The National Chamber would therefore fulfil the pricing and allocative functions which, under existing arrangements, were performed by the market mechanism. It would also perform the equilibrating role of matching the demand and supply of individual commodities and, in addition, it would, for Gray, determine how the national product was distributed. Thus, as regards the remuneration of labour, there would be 'fixed scales of payment for different employments, allowing something more than the average for some kinds of work, and something less than the average for other kinds'.[29] As for those engaged in the business of 'superintendence and of direction', the 'average wages of the [National Chamber's] agents … should always be a fixed sum, having a proper relation to the price of common labour'.[30] It would be the case, therefore, that 'every commercial member of the Social Society would be employed upon the principle of prescribed duty and prescribed reward. The hours of attendance would be fixed; the work to be performed, in cases of productive labour, would be of a defined quality.'[31] So the distribution of the national product would no longer be left to the vagaries of the market. It would now be consciously determined by reference to skill, responsibility and merit.

Finally, and crucially, the National Chamber, together with a National Bank, would play a fundamental equilibrating role at a macroeconomic level. With the institutions of his Social System in place, it would be by no means difficult to place the commercial affairs of society upon such a footing, that production would become the uniform and never failing cause of demand; or, in other words, that to sell for money may be rendered, at all times, precisely as easy as it now is to buy with money.[32]

Thus commodities would be priced according to the labour time they embodied, plus 'the percentage of profit, fixed by the Chamber of Commerce, to pay the various expenses of rent, interest of capital, management, salaries, depreciation of stock, incidents and all national charges'.[33] Labour notes would be paid to enterprises by the National Bank equivalent to that sum and these labour notes would, as Gray believed, furnish a demand commensurate with the value of what was supplied.[34] So 'money ... would increase as produce should be increased; money would decrease as produce should be redemanded or consumed and demand would ever keep pace with production'.[35] At both a macroeconomic and a sectoral level, therefore, the planners would be able to ensure the equilibration of supply and demand. The depression that afflicted the British economy, and with a particular intensity in the early 1830s, would in this way become a thing of the past.

Gray's *Social System* can be seen as displaying theoretical and prescriptive traits which were to characterise the work of other socialist political economists in the 1830s and 1840s.[36] In its reaction to his own earlier predilection for communitarianism it forms part of a tendency in the late 1820s and 1830s to look for solutions to working-class ills which eschewed the creation of a new moral world in microcosm and which envisaged the New Jerusalem in other than communitarian terms. Gray's reaction against the communitarianism of the *Lecture* is clearly manifest in the *Social System*, where he wrote that he was 'not anxious to rescue from oblivion the aforesaid pamphlet, which ... was merely an introduction to the present subject, and contained no attempt to explain how matters might be improved'.[37] Further in the *Social System* he sought to distance himself from the perfectibilism which he now saw as associated with communitarian socialism, emphasising that what he proposed 'ha[d] nothing to do with any speculative theories upon the perfectibility of man ... it requires merely a conventional plan of exchange, and a rational species of money; and ... merely that degree of rectitude of conduct which is essential to the existence of civilized society at all'.[38] There was no Owenite allusion in what was offered to the possibility of a revolution in the mind and character of the human race.

Also the focus of the *Social System* was in line with the increasing contemporary emphasis by the co-operative movement

and trades unions on the business of production. More specifically it reflected a stress by them on the need to secure ownership
and control over productive capacity, if the lot of labour were to
be radically improved. It is true that like most other early nineteenth-century British socialists Gray saw exploitation, and all its
associated evils, as rooted in unequal *exchange*. However, while
his critical attention was on the sphere of exchange, his concern
to socialise and rationalise the business of buying and selling led
him inexorably to consider the basis on which production was
organised and thence to discuss questions concerning the ownership and direction of productive power. Here Gray stressed the
need for a *national capital* and its conscious, centralised, social
direction by means of planning. As Marx wrote of Gray in his
Contribution to the Critique of Political Economy, 'although Gray
merely wants "to reform" the money evolved by commodity exchange,
he is compelled by the intrinsic logic of the subject-matter to
repudiate one condition of bourgeois production after another'.[39]

Finally, it is important to note the means by which the new
order would be created and those by whom it would be directed.
Here, while Gray allowed the possibility that working-class capital
accumulation might initiate the change, it was upon the initiative
of the capitalist class that his faith largely rested. It is they who
would come together voluntarily to relinquish ownership of what
they possessed in return for national annuities; it is from that class
too that the economic leaders, the technocrats of the new social
order, would emerge. In this respect, as we shall see, Gray clearly
differed from J.F. Bray and from those, like the syndicalists of the
Pioneer, who looked to the working class to provide both the
agency of change and the decision-makers of a transformed
economic and social order. But in this important respect Gray,
Bray and syndicalists, such as 'Senex', were similar and distinct
from the communitarians. They recognised the crucial importance of social ownership and control of *existing productive capacity*
as a means of achieving their objectives. They did not therefore
succumb to the notion that the existing sources and deployment
of economic power could be ignored.

This was to remain Gray's position in *An Efficient Remedy for
the Distress of Nations*, 1842, though in that work he was clearly
thinking more in terms of the nationalisation of the commanding
heights rather than the totality of the means of production. Thus
he argued that 'a section of government' should be appointed 'to
establish and control a great number of extensive manufactories
in various branches of the least speculative character'.[40] Other
areas of productive activity would be left to private entrepreneurs,
as would the retail trade. We have here, therefore, some notion of
a mixed economy, though one where the social ownership of

productive capacity is still of fundamental importance. It was only when he came to write his *Lectures on the Nature and Use of Money*, 1848, that Gray abandoned altogether the notion of public ownership, seeing macroeconomic disequilibrium as amenable to a technical, monetary solution.

John Francis Bray was born in Washington DC on 26 June 1809. His ancestors were, primarily, farmers and cloth manufacturers who had worked in or near Huddersfield for several generations, but his father had emigrated to the United States in 1805 and was to remain there until 1822. In that year, for reasons of his own ill-health, he returned with John to England, dying just a few days after his arrival in Leeds. Bray became apprenticed to a printer in Pontefract and, after continuing his apprenticeship at Selby, spent a period as an itinerant journeyman printer, before returning to Leeds to secure employment for a time (1833–34) on the *Voice of the West Riding*, one of the more notable of the many unstamped, working-class papers of the period.

It was during the early 1830s and as a result of his experiences as a journeyman printer that he first began to consider, write about and discuss social and industrial questions and, in particular, the impoverished condition and economic vulnerability of the labouring class. Between December 1835 and February 1836 he had published, in the *Leeds Times*, five 'Letters for the People' and, in November 1837, he delivered a series of lectures to the Leeds Working Men's Association, of which he was treasurer. Both Letters and Lectures prefigured the work for which he is now primarily remembered, *Labour's Wrongs and Labour's Remedy or, the Age of Might and the Age of Right*, which was published in weekly numbers in 1838 and as a whole in 1839.[41]

With Bray we have another writer who was emphatic as to the primacy of economic power and who saw its distribution as the key determinant of the material condition of labour. In this regard the governmental form taken by political authority was unimportant.

> The masses of all nations have been alike poor, and persecuted, and miserable, under republics as well as monarchies – under every known modification of government by the few and government by the many – which cannot but lead men to suspect that a mere form of government is not the secret enemy which devours them; and that, therefore, no government change can destroy this enemy.[42]

Consistent with this, he argued that the traditional programme of reforms articulated by political radicals would do little or nothing to improve the position of these 'masses'.

'Equal rights and equal laws', has long been the war-cry of the
working classes of Great Britain ... Some men, when they
speak of equal rights, mean thereby simply that there should be
universal suffrage, vote by ballot, and free admission to
Parliament; while others, advancing rather nearer to first principles, call for the complete subversion of the monarchy and
the establishment of a republic ... But an examination of the
subject will convince us, that if the working classes of the
United Kingdom should obtain any or all of the political
changes just mentioned, they would remain in almost the same
condition of poverty and ignorance and misery as they are at
present.[43]

This was so for two reasons. First, those who pressed for radical
political reform propounded remedies which merely scratched the
surface of labour's difficulties. They sought a reduction of
wasteful and corrupting government expenditure and a consequent reduction in the tax burden which labour shouldered.
However, as Bray saw it, 'even if every government burthen be
swept away and taxes abolished', 'the producers [would] be
almost as poor and ignorant and as hardworked as they are at
present'.[44] The fact was that the major exactions upon the
product of labour derived from the exploitative exercise of
economic, not political, power and could only be remedied by
measures which fundamentally altered the distribution of the
former.

Second, economic arrangements characterised by the wealth of
the few and the poverty of the many would 'effectually subvert all
equality of rights and laws, whatever may be the form of government established, and whatever may be the merely political power
placed in the hands of the working man'.[45] Even with access to
political power the existing distribution of economic power would
guarantee the perpetuance of labour's impotence. So, even if
political radicals were to advance a more effectual economic
programme than one which merely focused on the iniquities of
'Old Corruption', the political means of implementing it would
prove inadequate to the task. 'Thus whether we regard governmental change and the establishment of political equality either as
a means or as an end ... both reason and experience join in
showing us the utter worthlessness of such changes, either as
means or as ends.'[46] It was, indeed, the implicit and explicit
recognition of 'the insufficiency of political measures to remedy
social grievances' which had periodically led labour to seek 'relief
by the institution of trade societies and trade unions' i.e. by way
of organisations operating in the economic sphere and with a
measure of purchase on the sources of economic power.[47]

Rather than the political determining, or having the capacity to determine, the economic, it was the distribution of economic power, deriving from the existing pattern of property ownership, which decided the limits of political authority, regardless of the constitutional framework within which that authority was exercised. 'Every form of government, and every social wrong', wrote Bray, 'owes its existence to the existing social system – to *the institution of property as it at present exists*'.[48] So the existing exploitative and impoverishing economic and social arrangements would 'necessarily produce governmental institutions imbued with [their] own spirit and characteristic of [their] own vileness and depravity'.[49] The latter must reflect the former: the character of the former determine the nature and objectives of the latter. For that reason, 'if we would end our [labour's] wrongs ... THE PRESENT ARRANGEMENTS OF SOCIETY MUST BE TOTALLY SUBVERTED'.[50] However, before considering what form Bray believed that subversion should take, it is necessary to consider what he saw as the definitive features of the economic system which made for labour's impoverishment in the 1830s.

Here Bray is at one with Hodgskin, Gray and Thompson in defining labour exploitation in terms of unequal exchanges. To understand the causes of working-class immiseration was to understand the nature and consequences of these.

> The subject of exchanges is one on which too much attention cannot be bestowed by the productive classes; for it is more by the infraction of this ... condition [equal exchanges] by the capitalist, than by all other causes united, that inequality of condition is produced and maintained, and the working man offered up, bound hand and foot, a sacrifice on the altar of Mammon.[51]

All wealth proceeded from labour. Capital, 'the vast accumulations now in Great Britain', was, therefore, 'neither the production of the labour of the present race of capitalists nor their predecessors, and [was] never given to them in exchange for any such labour'; so capital did not 'belong to the capitalists either on the principle of creation or the principle of exchange. Nor [was it] theirs by right of heirship; for having been produced nationally [it could] only justly be inherited by the nation as a whole.'[52] To purchase labour with capital involved, therefore,

> giv[ing] the working man, for his labour of one week, a part of the labour wealth they obtained from his the week before! ... The wealth which the capitalist appears to give in exchange for the workman's labour was generated neither by the labour nor

the riches of the capitalist, but it was originally obtained by the labour of the workman ... The whole transaction, therefore, between the producer and the capitalist, is a palpable deception, a mere farce.[53]

It was from such transactions that the existing inequality of wealth and power had arisen; it was these unequal exchanges which ensured that such a skewed distribution of economic power was perpetuated and it was that which rendered ineffectual any attempts to better the condition of labour by political means.

Now the point can be made, as it can with respect to the political economies of Hodgskin, Gray and Thompson, that, in contrast to Marx, Bray locates exploitation in the sphere of exchange rather than at the point of production. Yet Bray's formulation of the nature of exploitation is, at some points, remarkably similar to Marx's. Bray does not make the distinction between labour and labour power so crucial to the Marxian theory of labour exploitation. But he does distinguish between the units of labour time necessary to furnish a worker's subsistence and the labour time furnished by labour for his capitalist employer. 'The workmen have given the capitalist the labour of a whole year in exchange for the value of only half a year.'[54] Implicit in this is the notion of unpaid labour time and even that of a rate of exploitation or rate of surplus value. Further, Bray was clear that the opportunity to effect such unequal exchanges derived from the ownership of the means of production. Also, with Bray, the term 'capitalist' was stripped of any remaining 'Old Corruption' connotations. Money might play a part in the obfuscation of value, and thence the exploitative nature of exchange, but the power of the capitalist lay not in money juggles but in the ownership of productive capacity. It was 'the very position of the capitalist, as the exclusive holder of the soil, as exclusive possessor of the national accumulations, and as the exclusive controller of the labour of the people' which enabled him to 'rais[e] profits or lower wages'.[55] The fact was that 'under the present social system the whole of the working class are dependent upon the capitalist or employer for the means of labour'; it was this 'inequality of possession' of the means of producing which gave 'man this dominion over his fellow man'.[56]

The power to exploit resided in the ownership of the means of production; it was derived from the ownership of land and the accumulation of capital; it was exercised through the purchase and the control of labour and it was the unequal exchanges which eventuated which established an unbridgeable social gulf and irremediable social antagonism between capitalists and labourers, employers and employed. In such an economic context

the capitalists and employers ... will always have interests
opposed to those of the producers at large. It is the interest of
the working man to acquire as much wealth as possible by
means of his own labour – it is the interest of the capitalist to
acquire as much wealth as possible by means of profit, or the
labour of other people; and as all profit must come from
labour, and as the wealth of the capitalist is but the accumulation of profit, the gain of the capitalist must be the loss of the
working man.[57]

Here, we have a pellucid articulation of the economic basis of
class conflict; an economic basis seen in terms of the relation of
the antagonistic classes to ownership of means of production. 'By
thus dividing society into two classes and *by keeping separate the
labour and the capital*, the ... capitalists are enabled by unequal
exchanges, to maintain the supremacy of their class over the
working class.'[58]

This was a gulf which could not be bridged by political means
and which, indeed, made a mockery of the belief that equal political rights could bring anything of substance in their wake for the
working class. For, 'under the existing social system, no form of
government can long remain effective of good to the people'. The
best, therefore, that could be hoped for, if universal suffrage and
the other demands of the political radicals were granted, was 'the
partial amelioration of the condition of the working class *as a
working class*'.[59] Class division on the basis of ownership/non-
ownership of the means of production, and the consequent
inequality of exchange between capitalists and labourer, would
remain.

As, then, the power to effect unequal exchanges and control
labour derived from ownership of the nation's productive means,
Bray was clear that to end exploitation and improve the material
position of labour it would be necessary that the means of production should pass into social ownership. Thus, 'it [was] necessary
... to the success of any social change, that the real capital of the
country should be possessed by the productive classes';

all the real capital of the country – the land, machinery, vessels,
and every other description of reproducible wealth, except the
personal property of individuals ... [should] be possessed and
controlled by society at large', while 'the occupations and
authority of the present capitalists and employers, in their indi-
vidualized capacity ... [should be] superseded.[60]

This transfer of productive capacity and power was to be effected
by one grand act of exchange whereby present owners would be

paid for the value of what they possessed by the issue of interest-bearing 'vouchers'. Like Gray, therefore, Bray suggested a variation on the theme of compensation by the issue of interest-bearing government stock. Further, his expectation was that these vouchers/government stocks would be rapidly redeemed and that, therefore, the charge upon labour would be short-lived. Thus 'assuming ... that all parties are willing to sell and to buy on the terms proposed – that the capitalists receive their vouchers and give up their property ... the whole of the two thousand millions debt could be wiped off within twenty years'.[61] Then, truly, the means of production would be socially owned and the material basis for exploitation and social antagonism removed.

Yet, if ownership was vested in society as a whole, social control of the means of production would operate at a number of levels. At the most basic level there would be collectively organised 'joint stock enterprises', the returns from whose productive activity would be shared equally amongst the workforce both in the form of wages and profits. On wages, Bray reasoned that as, under the division of labour, the contribution of each labourer was equally necessary to the business of production, so each should be equally rewarded.[62] Thus there is an egalitarianism in *Labour's Wrongs* that is manifestly absent from *The Social System*. Also, while the ownership of productive capacity was formally vested in society, Bray clearly saw workers as, in some sense, 'shareholders' of their respective joint stock enterprises. In this context Bray wrote of a 'joint stock modification of the principle of community of possessions'. Indeed, it was because workers were shareholders that they had a collective interest in making such companies succeed. In contrast to existing economic arrangements the 'opposition of interests does not exist in joint stock companies. If one shareholder gain or lose anything by a company, all the other shareholders do so likewise.'[63] In terms of reward this would mean that once all charges on national capital[64] had been met, workers would share in the surplus that remained.

So 'society' would, as envisaged by Bray, become 'one great joint-stock company, composed of an indefinite number of smaller companies, all labouring, producing and exchanging with each other on terms of the most perfect equality'.[65] The basis of that exchange, and of the currency which would be issued to facilitate it, would be labour time. Thus, like Gray, Bray also saw socialist exchange relations as proceeding in the same manner as those conducted by the Birmingham and London equitable labour exchanges of the early 1830s. Given all this, exploitation must cease. The labour cost of production would, in every instance, determine value; and equal values would always exchange for equal values ... Each person would exchange the values he individually received [for labour], for commodities of the same value as his respective wages; and in no case could the gain of one man or one trade be a loss to another man or another trade.[66]

However, while society would be 'composed' of these joint stock companies and while they would enjoy a measure of autonomy and be 'superintended by [their] managers and overlookers as at present', they would, none the less, be subject to the control of 'general and local boards, that would regulate production and distribution in gross'.[67] Thus 'by means of general and local boards of trade' and through the medium of

directors attached [by these boards] to each individual company, the quantities of the various commodities required for consumption – the relative value of each in regard to each other – the number of hands required in various trades and descriptions of labour – and all other matters connected with production and distribution, could in a short time be as easily determined for a nation as for an individual company under the present arrangements.[68]

Using 'statistics of every kind' which 'would acquire a degree of correctness and perfection such as they can never attain to under the existing system', these boards would make decisions in relation to demand, price, output and resource allocation for an industry or trade or firm which, in the context of a market economy, would be the unplanned outcome of the forces unleashed by self-interested activity. 'Production and distribution [would be] *regulated throughout society at large* – being alternately increased, or decreased, or turned into new channels as the exigencies of society require.'[69] As with Gray, therefore, the idea of planning, of the conscious social control of economic activity, is central to Bray's conception of a socialist economy. Only the existence of 'a power capable of regulating and adjusting the movements of society as a whole ... directing all efforts, in one harmonious flow, to a well-defined and proper end' would rectify the waste and inequity which resulted from the anarchic operation of a putatively competitive market.[70]

Also, in proposing the creation of a National Bank, Bray was again looking to an institution which would play a regulatory and planning role; ensuring that a labour currency expanded *pari passu* with the results of labour's productive activity. This, together with the remuneration of labour according to the time it expended on production, would eliminate those economic depressions resulting from deficiency of demand which had afflicted the British economy with particular severity since the end of the Napoleonic Wars.

The 'general and local boards of trade', which would fulfil a planning role, would be 'comprised of the most able and business-like men that can be found'. This suggests a techno-cratic/meritocratic solution to the problem of economic leadership similar to that advanced in John Gray's *Social System*. Yet, in contrast to Gray, Bray is clear that 'the members of [these boards] ... would be elected by communities'.[71] Bray introduced, therefore, a democratic element into his conception of the way in which a socialist economy would be organised. Further, as we have seen, while Bray discounted the efficacy of universal suffrage as a means of removing the economic and social ills which labour suffered; such an extension of the franchise being 'neither neces-sarily accompanied with, nor productive of equal rights'. He nevertheless believed that 'no equality of rights can be enjoyed by a nation without the accompaniment of universal suffrage'. Thus Bray's prescriptions for a socialist commonwealth had a strongly democratic flavour.[72]

Bray wrote of his proposed socialist commonwealth that it represented 'not an introduction of new principles and modes of action, but simply the application of existing principles and modes to a new object'.[73] On the surface this seems a strange assertion. It sits uneasily beside the statement that 'competition could have no existence in a change like this', the taking of the nation's productive capacity into public ownership, the socialisa-tion of exchange relations and the substitution of planning for the anarchy of the market.[74] Yet when juxtaposed to the prescriptive ideal of communitarian socialists there are important senses in which what Bray said was correct. Communitarian socialists thought in terms of a retreat from an old immoral world, leaving the ownership of existing productive capacity intact, to a world constructed *de nouveau* on a largely self-sufficient agrarian basis, with output distributed on the basis of need not effort. Bray looked to a transfer of the existing means of production to social ownership, while leaving the existing structures of production in place. In a sense, therefore, production would proceed on the same material basis as before. There would be no need for retreat in the direction of agrarian self-sufficiency. The prevailing balance between industry and agriculture could be maintained and thence the benefits of industrialisation secured for the community as a whole. There would be no immediate reconstitu-tion of society on communitarian lines but existing enterprises would continue to operate utilising existing labour and would, initially, be geared to producing what they had always produced. Labour would be rewarded, individually, on the basis of its productive efforts and society would be 'so constituted as to admit of individual property in productions in connection with common property in productive powers – making every individual dependent on his own exertions'.[75] Bray's socialist commonwealth was, therefore, one which, more completely than communitarian socialism, accommodated the realities of a Britain rapidly industrialising on the basis joint stock enterprises. In that important sense it was 'the application of existing principles and modes'. That should not, however, obscure the extent to which it represented a fundamental departure on grounds of economic principle as well as economic practice from the kind of competitive capitalism that was in the ascendant when Bray wrote.

CHAPTER 9

Chartist Socialism: a Social Democratic Political Economy

The wave of labour unrest and trades union activity which characterised the early 1830s came to an end in 1834 with the collapse
of the Grand National Consolidated Trades' Union in 1834 and
the defeat of the tailors' strike in the same year. Its final stages
also saw the collapse of those experiments in co-operative production which such trades union activity had inspired. In
consequence working-class aspirations for fundamental change,
which had taken a decidedly economic form in these years, now
assumed a more narrowly political character and the People's
Charter, published in May 1838, with its central demand for
universal male suffrage, became the focus of agitation and
remained so for a decade. However, 1848 was to see the third and
final abortive effort to effect a substantial measure of political
reform by way of petitioning Parliament and, in the aftermath of
that failure, a number of Chartists came to believe that if
Chartism was to be made a potent political force once again, it
would be necessary to fuse Chartist demands with an economic
programme clearly indicative of the kind of social transformation
that might be effected once political power had been won.

There was, though, a number of other reasons why 'Chartist
socialists' such as Bronterre O'Brien, Ernest Jones and G.J.
Harney saw the formulation of an economic programme as
imperative.[1] To begin with, in the early 1850s, the energies of the
working class were once again engaged in activities with essentially economic objectives. Specifically, the decade saw the growth
of producer and consumer co-operatives and also a number of
major industrial disputes.[2] Chartist socialists such as Jones and
Harney might have believed that trade unionism and co-operatives by themselves represented energy and resources expended to
little effect but they also recognised the degree of working-class
support which they elicited; the kind of support which was fast
ebbing from Chartism after 1848. To retrieve this, Chartism had
therefore to accommodate the material aspirations of labour
which the growth of such organisations expressed. It had to fuse
its political aims with a set of economic objectives which held out
the prospect not just of political empowerment but also of a

consequent marked improvement in labour's economic position.
Chartist politics and political economy had to be integrated and,
to secure the support of the working class, it was believed that
that political economy had to be recognisably socialist.[3] As Ernest
Jones put it in an 'Address to the People' published in the
Northern Star in August 1850:

> I believe it necessary that the practical and social results of the
> Charter should be laid before the public. I believe that the less
> enlightened portions of the working classes feel little sympathy
> with political rights, unless they can be made to see the results
> in social benefits; I believe that they do not yet fully understand
> the connection link between POLITICAL POWER AND
> SOCIAL REFORM.[4]

Or, as it was phrased in the *Programme* adopted by the Chartist
Convention of 1851,

> the Convention is of the opinion ... that we cannot claim or
> receive the support of the labourer, mechanic, farmer or trader,
> unless we show them that we are practical reformers ... that the
> Charter would confer on them a positive, immediate, and
> permanent benefit, and at once increase alike their comforts
> and resources.[5]

Of course, in the work of a writer such as O'Brien the economic
dimension had always loomed large and, over time, acquired a
socialist hue. O'Brien had read Hodgskin, Gray and Thompson
in the early 1830s and from his earliest writings in *Carpenter's
Political Letters* (1831) he had discussed the means by which
labour was exploited and the social and material consequences
which eventuated. For O'Brien political power had never been
simply an end in itself but a means, not only of removing the tax
and expenditure evils of 'Old Corruption', but also of eliminating
the income streams of 'profitmongers', landowners, 'moneymon-
gers' and all those who consumed without producing. O'Brien
was to refine and elucidate the means by which such objectives
were to be achieved in the late 1830s but we can already distinguish the broad outlines of what he proposed in his *Poor Man's
Guardian* editorials earlier in the decade. Thus an integration of
Chartist political objectives with an anti-capitalist political
economy was, in some measure, already available prior to 1848 in
the writing of O'Brien.

   Yet as regards the recognition of the need to combine the political programme of Chartism with an explicitly socialist political
economy, the events of 1848 were also crucial – not just those in

Britain, where the pursuit of the purely political objectives of the
Charter had proved abortive, but also events in continental Europe
and, in particular, in France. There universal suffrage, the key
component of the Charter, had been won but what had resulted
was not a legislature containing working-class representatives and
advancing working-class interests but, as one contemporary
commentator put it, 'a chamber dominated by bankers, landlords,
army officers and others of the propertied classes'.[6] Further, when
measures advantageous to the working class had been implemented, such as the creation of Louis Blanc's *ateliers nationaux*,
these had been disowned and attacked by the 'people's' representatives. Thus Harney, in the *Democratic Review*, wrote that 'the
present lamentable state of France, should be sufficient to teach all
thinking men the folly of resting their hopes on a mere enlargement
of voting power, unless that enlargement be accompanied with, or
preceded by, a general popular knowledge of social evils and the
remedies for those evils'.[7] If such mistakes were not to be repeated
in Britain, then Chartism must become socialist as well as democratic or, as one contributor to the *Red Republican* phrased it:
'Chartism and red republicanism must henceforward be regarded
as synonymous.'[8] For this to happen it was necessary to formulate
a political economy of Chartist socialism.

A similar point was made by both Harney and Jones with
respect to the United States. There, as in France, democratic
republican rights had been won, but clearly,

> republican institutions [had proved to be] no safeguard against
> social slavery. Where a great difference between the posses-
> sions of one man and those of another is allowed to exist, no
> political laws can save the working man from wages-slavery;
> where free access to the means of production is denied, where
> that access is dependent on the will of a few rich men, it is
> always in the power of the latter to force that wages-slavery, by
> means of competition, down to the veriest point of misery.[9]

Political power might indeed be a *sine qua non* for social advance,
but unless wedded to economic power it was likely to provide a
set of formal rights which made little material difference to the
position of labour. As Harney saw it,

> a social revolution in America is a necessary and indispensable
> complement to the political revolution of '76. Should no such
> revolution or reformation, come to pass, the future of America
> cannot fail to be a copy of Europe at the present time – the
> community divided into two great classes: a horde of brigands,
> monopolizing all the advantages of society, and a multitude of

landless profit-ridden slaves, deprived of even the names of citizens and subjected to the control of omnipotent Wealth and rampant Privilege.[10]

What was wanted was not simply democracy but social democracy.

Yet if Chartism was indeed to be fused with a socialist political economy, that was to have as profound implications for the latter as the former. For, if Chartism now acquired a socialist economic programme, that programme had, as an integral element, the use of the political power which an implementation of the points of the Charter would make available. Thus the pursuit of social rights and social emancipation by purely economic or non-political means continued to be seen by these Chartist socialists as doomed to failure. This had been the credo of O'Brien in the *Poor Man's Guardian* and it was spelt out just as forcefully in the early 1850s. Ernest Jones in particular singled out both trade unionism and producer and consumer co-operatives for rough treatment. Trade unions must, inevitably, fail to attain their objectives. They must do so because they operated in a labour market where capitalism continually created a supply of labour surplus to its requirements. It did so through the elimination of small-scale units of production in agriculture and manufacturing, by mechanisation, by the addition of women and children to the workforce and by the lengthening of the working day and intensification of labour.[11] To maintain existing levels of wages let alone improve them was, therefore, an impossibility. Where the forces of supply and demand were weighted so heavily in favour of the capitalist, only the destruction of the wage system itself could improve the material position of labour. For that, political power was essential. Thus, as regards the trade union activity of the 'amalgamated machinists, engineers etc.', Jones wrote:

> it is not a palliative but a cure that we, the toiling slaves, require – not a mere botching and bolstering up of a bad vitiated system, but the power to supersede that system, and substitute a better: this power can be obtained only by introducing a political element into our movement.[12]

Further, in so far as trades unions did wield any power, they did so, for Jones, by creating an exclusive aristocracy of labour and thus by mirroring the kind of monopoly power which capitalists used to exploit the greater part of the labour force. As he put it in an 'Address to the Iron Trades':

> the monopolies of these 'societies' and 'unions', with their dictatorial trade regulations towards their poorer fellow-workmen,

have been some of the most oppressive, unjust and tyrannical on
record. They have estranged the feelings of the many, who were
unable, or not permitted, to enter their privileged and aristo-
cratic circle; they have been the fruitful seminary of that worst of
all aristocracies, the aristocracy of labour, they were hated by
those beyond their pale – and it is owing to this, as well as to the
fearful labour surplus, that the master-class find plenty of men
able and willing to supersede those haughty 'brothers'.[13]

The crucial point, however, was that, for the most part, trades
unions could not hope to be effective until political power was
used to reconstitute the economic basis of society and eliminate
the forces making for a permanent labour surplus.

Similarly, as regards the economic evils of capitalism, co-operatives could have only an ameliorative effect and that a temporary
and problematic one. It would be temporary because the capitalist had always at his disposal the means to destroy them. As
Jones wrote in a letter to E.V. Neale, one of the foremost proponents of producer and consumer co-operation in mid-nineteenth
century Britain,

> it rest[s] in the power of the great moneyed class to prevent
> and to destroy the associative movement wherever they choose
> – unless co-operation were backed by political power. I argue
> that they would do this, partly by restrictive and injurious laws
> – and partly by means of competition. For the co-operator
> would have to compete with the great capitalist, and the latter,
> as possessed of the larger capital, and, of consequence, enabled
> to buy and to manufacture cheaper than the co-operator,
> would be also enabled to undersell, and thus to destroy him.

If co-operation did manage to flourish it was simply because
'monopoly' had not yet found it expedient to effect its destruction
or, 'because [it] has not yet had time and means to absorb all the
channels of trade'.[14]

Where co-operatives did manage to survive the full competitive
onslaught of capitalist producers and wholesalers, it could only be
at the cost of abandoning those co-operative principles which
stressed the equitable remuneration of producers and a fair price
for consumers. Such co-operatives

> have got to compete with the capitalist who lowers his prices
> in competing with the co-operative manufacturer. The capit-
> alist compels all his wages slaves to work for less and the
> co-operative manufacturer is obliged to lower his profits in
> order to compete with the monopolist, who lowers his wages.[15]

Unsupported and unprotected in a competitive market dominated by large-scale capitalist producers, co-operatives could be picked off as and when profitability or other considerations necessitated. Without fundamental changes in existing economic arrangements and the legal framework within which co-operatives operated, they would inevitably fall victim to bankruptcy or to the abandonment of 'the true principles of associative labour'.[16] Such changes could only be effected through the acquisition and use of political power. Again, for Chartist socialists, the role of the state was crucial.

As regards the primacy of the role of the state in their political economy, it has been suggested that Chartists such as Harney and Jones may also have been influenced by the work of continental socialists and, in particular, those who had fled continental Europe to take refuge in Britain. Amongst these emigrés was Marx, with whom both Harney and Jones were acquainted and with whom they corresponded. A piece by Marx, on France, entitled 'June 29, 1848' appeared in Jones' *Notes to the People*, while Marx and Engels' *Communist Manifesto* first appeared in English, in November 1850, in four issues of the *Red Republican*.[17] Harney's *Democratic Review* (July 1849) also gave expression to the demands of the German Communist Party promulgated by Marx and Engels in February 1848. These had been published in the Swiss journal *Evolution* and were reprinted in the *Democratic Review* of July 1849 as the 'Manifesto of the Red Republicans of Germany'. In addition, it is likely that certain anonymous articles, appearing in the *Red Republican* and the *Democratic Review* in the early 1850s, were written by Engels.[18] Both Jones and Harney, fluent as they were in German, acquainted as they were with Marx and Engels and, more generally, the German emigré community, could not, therefore, have failed to have been aware of the central themes of the political economy articulated by Marx and Engels in the *Communist Manifesto* and elsewhere, nor ignorant of its demands for

> heavy progressive or graduated income tax ... centralization of credit in the hands of the state, by means of a national bank with state capital ... an exclusive monopoly ... [and] central-ization of the means of transport and communication in the hands of the state ... [and an] extension of factories and instru-ments of production owned by the state.[19]

Indeed, all of these were to loom large in the policy prescriptions of the Chartist socialists.

In terms of continental influences one should note too that the *Democratic Review* provided an outlet for the ideas of Louis Blanc. A series of articles appeared under the title 'Social reform, the principles and projects of Louis Blanc', while the same volume of the paper contained Blanc's *The History of Socialism, a Course of Lectures Delivered to French Workmen Residing in London.*[20] Also, Blanc's creation of the state-funded *ateliers nationaux* must have made an impression on the thinking of Chartists in the period, emphasising as they did the economic responsibilities of the state to the working class in general, and those whom capitalism had rendered redundant in particular.

Yet all that said there are good reasons for stating that, in general, the central features of the political economy of Chartist socialism were essentially homegrown and that the crucial influences on O'Brien, Harney and Jones were those of indigenous thinkers and traditions of thought. While the ideas of Blanc certainly circulated widely, their greatest impact was on those who saw producer co-operatives as an autonomous means of economically emancipating the working class and clearly the Chartist socialists were critical of such notions. Further, as regards the economic role of the state there is much, as we have seen, in indigenous socialist political economy from which the Chartist socialists might have derived inspiration. Although, therefore, it is putting it too strongly to say, as Schoyen does, that by the late 1840s 'the idea of state-socialism' had 'long been endemic in England',[21] it is none the less the case that a writer such as Bray did consider the state as an important means of effecting such a transformation in the economic life of the nation as would allow the attainment of socialist objectives. As we have seen too, both Bray and Gray also mooted the idea of a *National Bank.* In addition, the idea of imposing a 'heavy progressive or graduated income tax' to fund certain social welfare ends can be traced back at least as far as the second part of Tom Paine's *Rights of Man.* And, as regards the relationship of the state to the nation's productive resources, it will become apparent, when the economic programme of the Chartist socialists is considered in more detail, that they owed a considerable debt to the agrarian radicalism of Spence and Ogilvie, and that their ideas parallel in many respects those to be found in Senex's *Letters on Associated Labour.* Whatever the influence of continental thinkers, therefore, and however sensitive writers like Harney and Jones were to political developments on the continent and the trials and tribulations of European social democracy, the political economy of Chartist socialism had deep domestic roots.[22]

If, therefore, in the period after 1848 socialist political economy was used to transform Chartism into 'red republicanism' or, in another categorisation of the time, into 'Chartism and something more', it was also the case that Chartism, through its emphasis on the political, produced a socialist political economy in which the economic role of the state was paramount. Thus the 'People's Charter' remained 'the medium through which they [the working classes] must achieve their deliverance from social oppression'.[23] However, before reviewing the specifics of Chartist state socialism, it is important to consider the essential elements of their critique of mid-nineteenth-century capitalism, for that critique throws considerable light on the prescriptive dimension of their political economy.

What is striking about that critique is the considerable emphasis placed on the exploitative power conveyed by ownership of the means of production, both land *and* industrial productive capacity. That power had two aspects: first, it was the power to deny access to the means of labouring and, second, the power to create a permanent labour surplus. As Ernest Jones saw it,

> land and money-lords have it in their power to make what terms they like – because, holding land and machinery – they hold exclusive possession of the means to work ... the monopoly of land and the increase of machinery gives them the power of keeping the labour plentiful ... They must work if they mean to live; and therefore the capitalist can dictate starvation terms ... This is social wrong in its fundamental aspect.

Further,

> I assert that capital, being possessed of a monopoly of political and social power, uses that power so, as always to ensure the supply of hireable labour remaining greater than the demand – so as always to keep a competitive reserve in the labour market, by which to force wages down, and keep the wage-slave beneath the heel of capital.[24]

Also, Jones detailed just how ownership of productive capacity allowed the capitalist to create this labour surplus. Thus 'super-fluous' labour resulted from 'the large farm system ... spreading'; from 'machinery ... being introduced ... into agriculture', from 'mechanical power in manufacturing ... hourly increasing', because 'through the means of machinery women can do the work of men, and children the work of both' and, finally, due to the fact that 'work is harder now than it used to be'.[25] Given such developments and with such expedients available to ensure a supply of labour continually in excess of the normal requirements of capital, employers invariably had the whip hand and labour had, necessarily, to yield its services for subsistence wages.

This power to exploit, to 'dictate starvation terms', had also increased over time and would, as the Chartist socialists saw it, continue to grow in the future. Here they noted the importance of the centralisation of capital. 'The wholesale dealer destroys the small shopkeeper; the large estate annexes the little; the great capitalists ruin the lesser.'[26] This further weakened the relative bargaining power of labour. Quite simply 'the more wealth centralises, the less can individual industry contend with accumulated capital' and the inevitable consequence was an intensification of the pressures making for the impoverishment of labour, growing social polarisation and an exacerbation of class antagonism.[27] The 'social future that awaits us in England' was, therefore, one characterised by 'a few dozen immense capitalists, with nothing between them and the most abject race of working wage-slaves, except a very limited class of aristocracy of labour, employed by them as stewards, foremen, overlookers and overseers'.

> The riches of the rich will be gigantic – the poverty of the poor will be inconceivable. All the intervening layers, that now melt into each other ... will be swept away – and the severance of the two classes will stand naked in its horrid distinctness. Then tyranny will reign such as the world has never witnessed – not, perhaps, the tyranny of the law, but the TYRANNY OF SOCIAL CIRCUMSTANCES. A few rich oligarchs will virtually coerce everything ... political laws are a farce when social power rests in the hands of an enemy![28]

Given this view of the social and economic shape of things to come it is unsurprising that the Chartist socialists should have seen class interests as utterly irreconcilable. As Ernest Jones put it, 'the capitalists of all kinds will be our foes as long as they exist, and carry on against us a war to the very knife. Therefore they must BE PUT DOWN. Therefore we must have class against class'; 'we assert that the interest of the capitalist of land, money, or machinery, is decidedly hostile to that of the working-man and the small shopkeeper – that, therefore, the capitalist *must* be their bitter enemies – *must* seek to compass their ruin and prevent their emancipation and prosperity'.[29] There was, therefore, no possibility of reforming capital or ameliorating its excesses. To demand, for example, 'a fair day's wage for a fair day's work' was to ask for

> a golden slavery instead of an iron one. But that golden chain would soon be turned to iron again, for if you still allow the system of wages slavery to exist, labour must be still subject to capital, and if so, capital being its master, will possess the power and never lack the will to reduce the slave from his fat diet down to fast-day fare![30]

There could be no compromise with capital; its power must we destroyed and along with it the class system which entailed the abasement of labour to a subsistence wage. As G.J. Harney put it,

> it is not any amelioration of the most miserable that will satisfy us; it is justice to all we demand. It is not the mere improvement of the social life of our class that we seek; but *the abolition of those classes* and the destruction of those wicked distinctions that have divided the human race into princes and paupers, landlords and labourers, masters and slaves.[31]

It should be noted too that Harney was the first English writer to take from Marx the sociological term 'proletariat' in order to categorise and identify a class whose interests were necessarily antagonistic to those of the bourgeoisie.[32]

How, then, were social and economic arrangements to be reconstituted to eliminate the material basis of class and wage slavery? Given the increasing centralisation of ownership, the growth of monopoly power and the consequent production of a labour force surplus to capitalist requirements; given the exploitative purpose to which this concentrated ownership of the means of production was put and given the inefficacy of all autonomous, working-class remedies for labour's ills, Charter socialists saw the nationalisation of key productive resources, the state-promoted extension of public ownership and the nationalisation of the means of exchange as the only economic programme that would secure a lasting and substantial improvement in the material position of the working class.

First and foremost here was the nationalisation of the land. As Jones saw it, 'the first and fundamental source of wealth, is the LAND, and labour applied to it. Connected with this is the first and fundamental guarantee of SOCIAL RIGHT, THE NATIONALISATION OF THE LAND.'[33] The justification for this was, essentially, that furnished by Spence and Ogilvie. As it was put in the economic programme of the Chartist Convention of 1851: 'this Convention believes that the land is the inalienable inheritance of all mankind; monopoly is therefore repugnant to the laws of God and nature'.[34] O'Brien in particular was familiar with the work of these authors and, indeed, it was after reading Ogilvie's *Essay on the Right of Property in Land* in 1837, that he began to 'persistently preach' the policy of land nationalisation.[35] However, if Spence sought the parochialisation of land and Ogilvie its redistribution to peasant proprietors, the Chartist socialists looked to its ownership by the state. Thus in addition to the land already in its possession or over which control could be costlessly acquired, 'the state ... [should] be empowered to purchase land, for the purpose of locating thereon the population, as tenants, individually or in association, paying a rent-charge to the state'.[36] Such rent-charges were to be used for the additional acquisition of land, though the use of tax revenue was also envisaged. Here stress was laid on the productive consequences of such a use of government revenue and an important distinction was made between expenditure on current and capital account. Thus

> it must always be remembered that the mere fact of spending money does not, in itself, impoverish the spender; it always depends on whether the outlay is or is not for a reproductive object. In the same manner in which the people were drafted on the land, pauperism, disease and crime would be diminished; home trade would re-appear – in fine, taxation would fall and revenue would rise. Here then is the reproductive investment of capital.[37]

In opposition to the spirit of the age, therefore, state expenditure was seen neither as diverting resources to less productive purposes nor simply as ameliorating social ills but as a means of actively promoting economic activity and reducing the government expenditure necessary to cope with the social and material evils which industrial capitalism created. Like Keynes a century later, Jones grasped and articulated the paradox that an appropriate increase in government expenditure was an effective way to raise revenue and cut taxation.

As to the form which agricultural holdings would assume, while it is clear that the possibility of individual tenant farming was acknowledged, some kind of collective application of labour to land was both anticipated and favoured. Thus it was 'neither the small farm system, nor the large farm system, *as at present*, (and, indeed, as hitherto) developed, that we must strive for – but we must *bring large masses of labour to bear on proportionate masses of land* – this is co-operation, this is the only way to produce great results'.[38] Similarly, as one writer in the *Red Republican* saw it, after the land was 'declared national property', 'a great proportion of the population' would be formed into 'industrial armies organised for agricultural purposes'.[39] Thus the partial collectivisation of agriculture was an element in the Chartist socialist programme and here they put a considerable distance between themselves and O'Connor's Chartist Land Plan of the 1840s which sought to fund the proliferation of peasant proprietors.[40] The Chartist socialists had seen in the centralisation of productive activity a significant source of productivity gains. That, after all, was what gave capitalist enterprise a decisive competitive edge over its co-operative rivals. Account should therefore be taken of this when

the forms of social ownership best suited to the interests of society
were discussed.

The idea of nationalisation was also extended from the land to
other kinds of productive resource. In the case of mines and fish-
eries the extension was, as with Spence, a logical and an easy one.
Mines,

> after due examination and survey by public authority ... would
> [therefore] be let out to companies of actual workers by public
> tender, and what was realised over and above the rent paid to
> the State would go only to those who risked their lives in
> working them.

However, in addition to the nationalisation of such resources,
O'Brien argued that 'railroads should not be private property;
neither should canals, docks ... the supplying of gas, water etc.
Works of this sort designed for the use of the public, should be
constructed and executed only at public cost ... and the public
only should have the advantage'.[41] In effect, therefore, public
ownership should be extended to what we would now term the
public utilities or natural monopolies.

Harney went so far as to argue that 'O'Brien's proposals should
be boldly extended by the nationalization of manufactures',[42]
while a *Red Republican* correspondent wrote that 'land and
capital' should be seen as 'national not individual property'[43] and
the Chartist socialists, in general, certainly did envisage the extension of social ownership to a broad area of economic activity.
However, that extension was not always conceived of in terms of
nationalisation. Rather they thought too in terms of measures
which would facilitate the growth of producer co-operatives and
which would encourage the organisation of their operations in
such a manner as to give them a collective strength, identity and
purpose. That said if producer co-operation was to develop in this
way and flourish, it needed the assistance of the state. At the most
fundamental level co-operatives needed legal recognition so that
their funds would be protected. More importantly, if they were to
survive the competition of capitalist enterprises, the state must
furnish the credit necessary for their formation and rapid expansion. 'It is ... evident', wrote Jones,

> that, if the co-operative system is left to individual efforts,
> though those individuals act harmoniously together, it will
> advance far more slowly, and meet with counteracting influ-
> ences which it may be difficult, if not impossible, to overcome.
> *Co-operation should be made a state maxim, realised by the power of*
> *the state ...* therefore it is requisite, in the words of the [Chartist]

programme:- 'That a credit fund be opened by the state, for the purpose of advancing money, on certain conditions, to bodies of working-men, desirous of associating together for industrial purposes.'[44]

National credit was, therefore, to be provided for the creation and expansion of producer co-operatives. More generally as it was phrased in the propositions of O'Brien's National Reform League, 'national credit' was 'to be applicable to the requirements of individuals, companies and communities in all ... branches of useful industry as well as in agriculture'.[45] Thus,

> if ... [an individual] ... wishes to manufacture, he ought to have the means afforded to him of buying, or of making machinery, and of purchasing the new material, and for this purpose the state should advance to the working man out of the national revenue, on safe and equitable conditions, remunerative to the state itself, those funds which would enable him to maintain the requisite materials for manufacture.[46]

So the role of the state was crucial in promoting the socialisation of economic activity in ways other than nationalisation; while state-financed co-operative production could be used to drive a socialist stake into the heart of the capitalist system, eliminating private production and thence the very basis of the wage slavery suffered by the working class.

These writers also anticipated the producer co-operative movement evolving in a manner which made for a more collective and less competitive organisation of economic activity. A key problem with and for existing co-operatives was that they had to compete not just with capitalist enterprises but also with each other. Ideally, therefore, such co-operatives should be organised on a national basis according to trade or product. Producer co-operatives operating in competitive isolation could be 'an evil second only to that of ... monopoly';

> therefore, all future co-operative attempts should, until the complete readjustment of the labour question, be modelled on a national basis, be connected in a national union of which the different trades and societies should be localities or branches; and the profits, beyond a certain amount, of each local society, should be paid into a general fund, for the purpose of forming additional associations of working men, and thus accelerating the development of associated and independent labour.[47]

So while, in many areas of industry, it was believed that the social-isation of production should result from the proliferation and expansion of producer co-operatives, these should not operate independently but would be organised, promoted and financed on a national basis, i.e. in the kind of manner anticipated by Senex's *Letters on Associated Labour*. It is in such a context that Jones' exhortation to 'nationalise co-operation' should be under-stood. Clearly too the possibility of a single producer co-operative covering an entire industry or trade was also envisaged. Proposals from the miners of North Staffordshire published in Jones' *Notes to the People* asked miners to

> imagine the power you would have, if all the colliers and miners of Great Britain were to form ONE GREAT CO-OPERATIVE ASSOCIATION, having one common fund, one common centre, ... every month emancipating some wages-slaves ... from the thraldom of capital.[48]

Again, the intellectual pedigree of this idea may be traced back to the early 1830s.

In this context it was also noted by Chartist socialists that the centralisation of ownership by predatory competition had itself laid the basis for the kind of national social ownership and control of industry which they favoured. In this regard the concentration of production in a few hands was to be welcomed as permitting rapid progress in the direction of a socialised economy, once the working class possessed the requisite measure of political power. Thus

> to go forward is to *encourage every step that leads to centralisation*. The gold-kings are playing their own game in this respect. The task is not to destroy the centralisation of property – but to wrest that centralisation out of the hands of the few, and to vest it in the hands of the state ... From *national centralisation* all derive a benefit.[49]

There is here something profoundly Fabian about the political economy of the Chartist socialists; the Fabian socialists in the 1880s and 1890s were also to see the tendency to monopoly as part of an ineluctable progression, centralising economic power in a manner that facilitated the eventual extension of the national ownership, organisation and control of industrial activity.

Similarly Fabian was the notion that the social ownership of production, once established with state backing, would rapidly eliminate private enterprise by way of competition. Just as producer co-operatives unassisted by the state would be unable to compete with private producers, so those same producers would be impotent in the face of a competitive challenge from co-operative production organised on a national basis and supported by state resources. Capitalists would be 'competing against the resources of a nation – and the protecting influence of government'. Given this 'the present joint stock companies, great merchants, bankers, factory lords, landlords, coal kings, mine owners ... would all inevitably be ruined'. So, 'The slightest beginnings [of socially owned production] with government support, would be sure to absorb by reproduction all the capital and labour power of the country.'[50]

While, then, the extension of social ownership was to take a number of centralised and decentralised forms, these were all to a greater or lesser extent dependent on the support of the state. Political power was, therefore, *the* essential prerequisite of social progress. The expansion of producer co-operation, for example, would not happen on its own or, if it did, it would only be by departing from co-operative principles. National associations of producers might be formed but only after co-operative production had been expanded by national credit. Natural monopolies had to be taken into state ownership, as had key components of the nation's industrial infrastructure and, crucially, the land too must become the property of the state.

It was through this multifarious extension of social ownership that the state would, very largely, assume its crucial role as owner and controller of the means of production and the financing of this extension therefore received considerable attention from writers like O'Brien and Jones. Land, as we have seen, was to be purchased with funds raised by taxation and the rental income which accrued from publicly owned land would be used to extend national ownership further. Also, the purchase of productive capacity by producer co-operatives or individuals would be funded

> by advancing ... the sum of £10,000,000 per annum out of the Church income of £13,000,000; by advancing the sum of £26,000,000 per annum out of the interest on the National Debt ... by advancing the sum of £10,000,000 per annum out of the £16,000,000 for our naval and military expenditure ... by letting crown, church, poor and common lands.[51]

Also producer co-operatives, whether individually or nationally organised, would be expected to pay part of the surplus which accrued to them 'into a NATIONAL EXCHEQUER, for the extension of co-operation'.[52] Most importantly though, as already noted, there would be the credit advanced by the National Bank and its subsidiaries.[53]

The national control over finance, investment and productive capacity was also to be extended to the business of exchange and again, as with the national organisation of producer co-operatives, there are marked similarities here between the political economy of Chartist socialism and ideas circulating amongst the working class in the early 1830s; specifically those related to labour exchanges and the fundamental importance of effecting an equitable exchange of goods and services. Thus when O'Brien insisted that 'all commerce must be gradually reduced to equitable exchange on the principle of equal values for equal values, measured by a labour or corn standard', he was merely repeating what he had put forward in the *Poor Man's Guardian* almost two decades earlier.[54] That said, by the late 1840s, the idea of socialising exchange was more fully developed. Proposition 7 of O'Brien's National Reform League stated:

> that in order to facilitate the transfer of property or service and the mutual interchange of wealth among the people, to equalise the demand and supply of commodities, to encourage consumption as well as production, and to render it as easy to sell as to buy, it is an important duty of the State to institute in every town and city, public marts or stores, for the reception of all kinds of exchangeable goods, to be valued by disinterested officers appointed for the purpose, either upon a corn or a labour standard.

It would be on this basis that goods would be exchanged and 'the equitable principle of equal labour for equal labour' made to prevail.[55] Exchanges conducted in this manner would eliminate the possibility of exploitation, they would ensure at a micro- and a macroeconomic level the equation of supply and demand and they would exorcise the dissimulation and chicanery which characterised contemporary exchange relations. Exchange would no longer be a cause of antagonism, angst and social oppression, and the waste of labour attendant upon a proliferation of competing retail outlets would also cease. In such a proposed socialisation of exchange there was much here which was redolent of Gray and Bray.

One further responsibility was to be given to the state by the Chartist socialists and that was to provide adequately remunerated work for all who sought it.[56] Most obviously the state would offer this to the unemployed, but it was also envisaged that state employment would also be available to all those who were forced to accept employment at an exploitative level of wages. Such a system of state employment might be made, it was believed, the basis of a new poor law or, more accurately, a minimum wage

law, which was what a poor law worthy of the name should be.
Here it was acknowledged that attempts made in the past 'to fix
a minimum by law' had usually failed. But success might now 'be
achieved indirectly and without oppression'. Previously the
labourer had been forced to accept whatever wage the monopolist
of 'the means of labour' deemed appropriate. Such 'compulsion'
being 'as strong as if armed men dragged their slave to the factory
door'. A true poor law 'might prevent this, and might place it at
the workman's option to accept or not to accept the master's
terms'. Thus 'the poor-law might interpose' when the wage
offered to labour fell below some acceptable minimum level and
it might do so by 'always providing employment, at a certain scale
of remuneration'. 'Thus it [would be] in the power of a good poor
law to do that which no direct, prohibitive, and restrictive law has
been able to effect – to fix a minimum, below which it would be
impossible for wages to fall.'[57] This was clearly an interim
measure; a staging post *en route* to the New Jerusalem. But it was
also a crucial one in that in employing surplus labour and setting
a defensible minimum wage it would significantly erode the
bargaining power of capitalist employers.

   Commentators have seen the political economy of Chartist
socialism as prefiguring the social democracy of a later period in
Britain. Thus Schoyen has written that by 1850

> the Chartist movement had emerged as Britain's first avowedly
> social democratic party – that is, a party which aimed at the
> achievement of socialist measures through political means. A
> 'declaration of social rights' immediately adopted by the
> National Executive called for the nationalization of the land,
> mines and fisheries, the extension of state credit to all, a 'just
> and wise system of currency and exchange'.[58]

Similarly, John Saville has written of Ernest Jones that 'it was one
of [his] ... great achievements ... that after 1848, appreciating the
"connecting link" between "politics" and "economics", he wrote
into the Charter the assumptions and the social programme upon
which the modern socialist movement has been largely built'.[59]

   In support of such assessments it is certainly the case that the
nationalisation of the land, the public utilities and the nation's
industrial infrastructure, point in the direction of late nineteenth-
century social democracy as, in some respects, does the idea of
using national credit to extend social ownership and support
nationalised or socially owned enterprises. The idea of producer
co-operatives banding together in national associations and
organising production and distribution on such a basis may also
be seen as presaging the ideas of later writers and, in particular,

those of the early twentieth-century guild socialists. Yet, for all that, the political economy of the Chartist socialists has a Janus-like quality. They did, in some measure, anticipate the shape of socialist political economy to come. The very fact that O'Brien's work was reprinted in the 1880s shows that socialist writers in that period, a period characterised by growing support for a more statist approach to socialist advance, believed that O'Brien had something of importance and of contemporary relevance to say. Also, through his impact on writers like M.J. Boon, as well as through the republication of his work, O'Brien's views actually fed into and helped shape state socialist currents of economic thinking in the last third of the nineteenth century. But there is too a backward-looking dimension to their political economy. Their ideas on land are clearly inspired by those of Spence and Ogilvie, and they really have very little to add to the arguments of those writers against its untrammelled private ownership. Further, their whole emphasis on the nationalisation of land also reflected a view of agriculture which, on many occasions, could be overtly physiocratic and anachronistically stress (given the rapid industrialisation of nineteenth-century Britain) the primary importance of the agricultural sector. For Jones, 'food [was] the staple wealth'; 'the earth itself [was] the fundamental capital'.[60] He therefore regretted 'the land's desertion for the loom'. Similarly, O'Brien saw 'the surplus of agricultural produce' as 'the REAL CAPITAL which sets the artisans and handicrafts to work'.[61] While, therefore, their socialist political economy was undoubtedly applicable to an industrialising economy, there are reasons for believing that such an economy was not one that always informed their vision of the socialist future and that, on the contrary, they carried into the mid-century period some of that anti-industrial bias which, as we have seen, can be found in earlier socialist political economy.

Further, their views on the socialisation of exchange, the need to exchange equal values and the importance they attached to the value of goods reflecting the labour that they embodied, were derived from the socialist economic theorising and the labour exchange practice of the 1820s and 1830s. The works of Gray, Bray and Owen are all important here and, in the case of O'Brien in particular, Thomas Hodgskin's *Labour Defended*. As with these earlier socialist and anti-capitalist writers, the Chartist socialists also saw exploitation as originating in the sphere of exchange and the socialisation of that sphere was, necessarily, a key component of their prescriptive political economy.

The stress on the need to organise producer co-operatives in national associations must also be seen as in large measure inspired by the experience of the early 1830s. Certainly the responsibilities given to these associations to organise production and distribution were much the same as those proposed by Senex in the *Letters on Associated Labour*. In the *Letters* too we can find the aim of destroying the opposition of private entrepreneurs by way of competition. What was distinctive about the later proposals, however, was the fundamental financial role given to the state in supporting and extending producer co-operation. In the final analysis, though, their emphasis upon the acquisition of political power as the means of effecting a 'Social Revolution'[62] does, to a large extent, set these writers apart and does allow us to see in their writing the origins of the kind of social democratic political economy which was to emerge in Britain later in the century and which was to form the basis of the kind of economic programme which the Labour Party was later to seek to implement.

This stress on the political means of implementing a socialist economic programme was in part, of course, a consequence of their participation in the Chartist movement. But it must also be seen as deriving from a particular conception of the state; a conception which clearly differentiated them from an earlier generation of political radicals and from the kind of Cobbettian political radicalism which continued, in some measure, to infuse and inspire Chartism in the 1838–48 period. Prior to 1832 the fundamental charge against the state was that it abused its revenue-raising authority to finance the corruption involved in a system dependent upon sinecurists and placemen, while exploiting its power over the monetary system to enrich jobbers, brokers and financial interests in general. However, after 1832, it became apparent, to some at least, that state power was being directed to different ends. Old corruption still lived but now the charge against government was also often made that it represented and fostered the interests of profitmongers, factory lords, coal kings and mine owners. A new demonology emerged; or, at least, substantial additions were made to the old one. In addition, those who found a place in that demonology were increasingly defined according to their economic and not their political role. If, therefore, the essence of old corruption was the use of state power over resources to bolster a corrupt political system, the essence of the post-reform polity was seen as the use of power to influence and alter the economic system so that it legitimised and enhanced the economic authority which capital exercised over labour. The Poor Law Amendment Act was, for many, the most obvious case in point. The lessons to be drawn from this were various, but one in particular was clear. State power once acquired *could*, manifestly, be used to advance the material interests of a particular class. The desire for the suffrage was, therefore, no longer simply a desire to purge the system of grinding taxation and wasteful and corrupting expenditure. Rather it was the wish to secure the means of effecting a fundamental shift in the balance of economic power in favour of labour. This was the essence, and a distinctive essence it was, of the political economy of Chartist socialism.[63] The aim of effecting 'through Universal Suffrage, THE ABOLITION OF CLASSES AND THE SOVEREIGNTY OF LABOUR'.[64] That was what set it apart from almost all of what had gone before and that is what was truly significant in its legacy to the future.

Conclusion

What one sees in the period 1775–1850 is the articulation of a multiplicity of political economies which sought both to interpret the experience and express the interests of the working class. That there were many and not one reflects the varied nature of that experience which was, in part, a function of the profound economic and social changes which occurred in these years. Many economic and social historians are now at pains to stress the incremental character of these developments and the gradualness of the transition to an industrial society which occurred in this period, but the fact remains that while, in 1750, the dominant sector of the British economy was agriculture, by the mid-nineteenth century it was manufacturing. The sources of economic power which confronted Ogilvie and Spence were not those with which O'Brien and Jones had to reckon; nor were the causes of working-class impoverishment during the revolutionary and Napoleonic Wars the same as those that Thompson, Gray and Bray sought to elucidate after 1815. The sources of the discontent which fuelled the 'bread and blood' riots in East Anglia in 1816 were not the same as those that fired the co-operative and trade union movements of the early 1830s. The lineaments of the economic world inhabited by the Spitalfields silk weavers were different from those of factory workers of the mid-century period. The political economies formulated for the working class spoke to and reflected this multifarious experience.

Those of Spence and Ogilvie identified the agrarian roots of economic and political power which made for the subservience of labour in eighteenth-century Britain. Cobbett's 'Old Corruption' highlighted the manner in which financial capital seized the opportunities provided by war to marry its fortunes to those of a landed interest which, in its own right, was doing well out of the conflict. The moral economists spoke to the experience of those whose interests had seemed to be protected by ethical and customary norms which gave order and equity to economic life, but who, in the post-1815 period, saw those norms eroded by the strengthening blast of market forces. Both communitarian and state socialist political economy can be seen as differing ways of reconstructing that order. Both clearly attracted the support of an artisanate whose status and material condition were frequently threatened by the growth of a competitive market economy; both offered certainty and stability and, in the prescriptive articulation of their theories of value, they gave some theoretical substance to notions of a just price and fair remuneration. That said, while there was a tendency in communitarianism to see in land owner- ship the primary means of labour's emancipation and in autarchy the manner in which the demons of the old competitive, immoral world might be exorcised, writers such as Gray and Bray proceeded along very different lines. With Bray and Gray, British socialist political economy crossed a Rubicon; in their work there was an acceptance of the permanence and growing importance of industrial power and the realisation of the need for it to be consciously harnessed to social purposes if the material condition of labour was to be improved. For these writers economic devel- opment had arrived at a point, in Britain, where the power that derived from industrial capital could not be ignored by any retreat to the essentially pastoral sanctuary of co-operative communities. James Morrison, J.E. Smith and others writing in the early 1830s were of a similar mind. They also saw the need for the working class to secure the means of production for its own use. It too eschewed the siren call of communitarian sanctuary. But its vision was of a decentralised socialism in which we can detect the outlines of a political economy which was to be more fully devel- oped by guild socialists and syndicalists at the turn of the century.

With the Chartist socialists we have a fusion of both statist and syndicalist elements with the nationalisation of land, natural monopolies and industrial infrastructure, the national manage- ment of the currency and a national employment policy, together with a preparedness to countenance and, indeed, encourage the growth of producer co-operatives. Thus, in the 1830–50 period, we see in Britain the articulation of political economies which stressed the need for the social ownership of the ever more powerful means of production which served industrial capitalism and we see too, in embryo, the very different conceptions of public ownership and socialist economic organisation which were to dominate socialist economic debate for the next century and a half – the democratic as against the technocratic management of a socialist economy; the statist as against the syndicalist basis of social ownership; the decentralised as against the central organ- isation of economic life under socialism.

All this is not to suggest that an explanation of the distin- guishing theoretical characteristics of the differing anti-capitalist and socialist political economies of the period may simply be read off from the evolution of nascent industrial capitalism. There is, of course, no uncomplicated correspondence of this kind between material base and ideological superstructure. An emphasis on the primacy of land as a productive resource or deployment of the presuppositions and discourse of moral economy are not confined to the period when the former was the major factor of production or the latter was under critical attack. Both were to persist throughout the period in the political economies which sought to articulate the interests of the working class. Land looms large in the social democratic political economy of Harney and Jones and moral economy notions permeate ideas on economic planning advanced by Bray and Gray.

None the less an understanding of the economic developments which characterised the period goes a long way to explain the changing nature of late eighteenth/early nineteenth-century anticapitalist and socialist political economy. It throws light on the shifting angle of critical attack on existing economic arrangements; it explains, in some measure, the changing explanations of labour's impoverishment which writers advanced; it helps us understand the economic demonology which they constructed and how that altered over time; it also allows us a more nuanced reading of their work and gives us a greater sensitivity to the concepts they deployed and the language they used. Specifically, as regards this last point, an awareness of the changing character of industrial and agrarian capitalism in this period engenders a realisation that similar economic and sociological concepts were used to do very different analytical jobs and carried with them very different implications and connotations according to when and by whom they were deployed. Hodgskin's use of the term 'capitalist' has a different sociological content and involves a differently angled critical attack from 'capitalist' as used by Cobbett or for that matter 'capitalist' as deployed by Harney and Jones. Only an understanding of the nature of the economic realities with which they are seeking to come to terms will provide us with an insight into this. Similarly, an understanding of how anticapitalist and socialist political economists use such terms as 'interest', 'profit', 'monopoly', 'value', 'middleman', is heavily dependent on an awareness of economic context. The absence of such an appreciation carries with it a number of dangers, but in particular a tendency to interpret a similarity of discourse as involving a continuity of critical analysis. Thus the fact that Cobbett, Hodgskin, Bray and O'Brien rail against 'middlemen' or 'monopoly' becomes reason enough to interpret their political economies as part of the same tradition of political radicalism. In fact, because their focus is on different aspects of a changing economic reality, these terms or concepts serve very different critical functions from those that they perform in the political economy of political radicalism.

A central purpose of this book has been to show how varied those traditions are and to show how they could all speak with force and authority to different elements of a differently circumstanced working-class constituency at different times. Yet if what we have are political econom*ies* for the working class, the constituency may none the less still be seen as singular rather than plural. If the different political economies which have been considered in this book articulate a varied working-class experience of emergent industrial capitalism, they none the less embody common components which imply that significant elements of that experience were shared. All highlight the increasing concentration of economic power – whether through enclosure, the spreading tentacles of the Pitt system, the growing capacity of middlemen to manipulate market exchange or the concentration of the ownership of industrial capital. Conversely, all expatiate on the growing powerlessness of labour and the tendency to increasing impoverishment which resulted from this. All also sought to answer the question of why the many were poor.

Finally, these political economies all conveyed a sense of the growing volatility and uncertainty of economic life, whether as the consequence of an increasing tendency to macroeconomic depression or as a result of marked and rapid changes in the value of money. Prescriptively, the corollary of this was a search for stability, security and certainty. Of course the structures of an economic world possessed of such characteristics were differently constructed by different writers, but the aspirations which the constructive dimension of their political economies embodied were markedly similar. What they looked for was an economic order where the centrality of labour in the production of wealth was reflected in its status, the power which it wielded and the material conditions it enjoyed; an order where it ceased to be a mere commodity, factor of production or cog in the productive machine but possessed the capacity to control its own economic destiny. What all wanted was an economic world which was consciously ordered and stable, where the status and condition of labour were not under constant threat and where change was controlled by labour itself with its interests to the fore. For only in such an economic order could the real rights of man finally be secured.

Notes

Preface

1. T. Spence, *The Restorer of Society to its Natural State*, London: 1801, Letter 14, in H.T. Dickinson (ed.), *The Political Works of Thomas Spence*, Newcastle upon Tyne, Avero: 1982, 92, hereafter *PWS*.
2. The chapter on William Cobbett does, however, look at one writer who saw in the political rights to be obtained by parliamentary reform, the essential means by which labour might fundamentally improve its material condition.

Chapter 1

1. B.R. Mitchell, *British Historical Statistics*, Cambridge: Cambridge University Press, 1988, 822.
2. P. Deane and B.R. Mitchell, *An Abstract of British Historical Statistics*, University of Cambridge, Department of Applied Economics, Monographs, 17, Cambridge: Cambridge University Press, 1971, 142–3.
3. Mitchell, *British Historical Statistics*, 103.
4. P. Jupp has written of 'a landed elite, estimated variously at between six thousand and ten thousand families from ducal to gentry'. 'The landed elite and political authority in Britain, c.1760–1850', *Journal of British Studies*, 29, 1990, 54.
5. Ibid., 56.
6. Wordie has argued that it was in the period 1600–1760 that a good 28 per cent of England was enclosed. J. Wordie, 'The chronology of English enclosure, 1500–1914', *Economic History Review*, 36, 1983, 494; ibid., 483.
7. J. Chapman, 'The extent and nature of parliamentary enclosure', *Agricultural History Review*, 35, 1987, 28. 'Such a figure considerably exceeds those given by many previous authorities ... The total of six million acres which has been widely used, for example, by Chambers and Mingay and McCloskey, represents an understatement of almost 18 per cent', ibid. M.E. Turner has provided an estimate of 6.8 million; see ibid., 29. J.M. Neeson, *Commoners: Common Right, Enclosure and Social Change in England, 1700–1820*, Cambridge: Cambridge University Press, 1996, 329; J.D. Chambers and G.E. Mingay (eds), *The Agricultural Revolution, 1750–1880*, London: Batsford, 1966, 77.

8. Neeson, *Commoners*, 5.
9. G.E. Mingay, 'The size of farms in the eighteenth century', *Economic History Review*, 14, 1961/62, 470.
10. M.E. Turner, 'Cost, finance and parliamentary enclosure', *Economic History Review*, 34, 1981, 236–48; K. Snell, *Annals of the Labouring Poor, Social Change and Agrarian England, 1660–1900*, Cambridge: Cambridge University Press, 1985, 191; 'Probably many cottagers sold such plots to the neighbouring farmers rather than go to the expense of fencing them and thus peasant proprietorship at the lowest level declined', Chambers and Mingay, *The Agricultural Revolution*, 97.
11. Neeson, *Commoners*, 254.
12. Chambers and Mingay, *The Agricultural Revolution*, 92.
13. Neeson, *Commoners*, 251.
14. Snell, *Annals of the Labouring Poor*, 142.
15. Cambers and Mingay, *The Agricultural Revolution*, 84.
16. J.V. Beckett, 'Land ownership and estate management', in G.E. Mingay (ed.), *The Agrarian History of England and Wales, 1750–1850*, Cambridge: Cambridge University Press, 1989, Vol. 6, 620, 621; see also *Commoners*, 290.
17. Mingay, *Agrarian history*, 621.
18. E.L. Jones, 'Agriculture, 1700–80', in R. Floud and D. McCloskey (eds), *The Economic History of Britain since 1700*, Vol. 1, Cambridge: Cambridge University Press, 1981, 75. For agricultural labourers food price inflation and poor harvests in 1795–96 and 1799–1801 made wages, for the greater part of these periods, 'inadequate to purchase even the wheat component of a wheat-based diet', R. Wells, 'The development of the English rural proletariat', in M. Reed and R. Wells (eds), *Class Conflict and Protest in the English Countryside, 1700–1880*, London: Cass, 1990, 35.
19. Jones, 'Agriculture, 1700–80', 75.
20. See M. Reed, 'Class and conflict in rural England: some reflections on a debate', in M. Reed and R. Wells (eds), *Class Conflict and Protest*, 8.
21. A. Charlesworth, 'The development of the English rural proletariat' in M. Reed and R. Wells (ed.), *Class conflict and protest*, 62.
22. P. Ashraf, *The Life and Times of Thomas Spence*, Newcastle upon Tyne: Graham, 1983, 11.
23. On this see T. Knox, 'Thomas Spence: the trumpet of Jubilee', *Past and Present*, 76, 1977, 83; and T. Parsinnen. 'Thomas Spence and the origins of land nationalization', *Journal of the History of Ideas*, 34, 1973, 137n.
24. T. Spence, *The Important Trial of Thomas Spence*, London: 1807, 27; T. Knox, 'Thomas Spence', 86.
25. See H.T. Dickinson, 'Introduction', *PWS*, viii. Murray used the term 'Common Estate' in his *The Contest*, Newcastle upon

Tyne, 1774, a work which, among other things, discussed the issues involved in the threatened enclosure of Newcastle Town Moor. 'This doctrine, that every individual has the right to life, and therefore to sustenance, was deeply rooted in western political culture by the late eighteenth century.' W. Stafford, *Socialism, Radicalism and Nostalgia: Social Criticism in Britain, 1775–1830*, Cambridge: Cambridge University Press, 1987, 103.

26. Quoted from Ashraf, *The Life and Times of Thomas Spence*, 25.
27. Quoted from ibid., 40.
28. Ibid., 18.
29. Ibid., 21.
30. As Parsinnen has written of Spence, 'his advocacy of parochial autonomy, secret balloting and a militia were typical of the eighteenth century commonwealthman's mistrust of the central government', 'Thomas Spence', 137.
31. It was to appear again in 1795 in *Pig's Meat*, Vol. III and as *The Meridian Sun of Liberty* in 1796.
32. T. Spence, *The Real Rights of Man*, London: 1795, *PWS*, 1; T. Spence, *The End of Oppression*, London: 1795, *PWS*, 34; ibid., 35.
33. Spence, *The Real Rights of Man*, 1; T. Spence, *The Restorer of Society to its Natural State*, London: 1801, *PWS*, 70; T. Spence, *The Rights of Infants*, London: 1797, *PWS*, 47.
34. Spence, *The Real Rights of Man*, 2; Spence, *The End of Oppression*, 35.
35. Spence was also scathing about Paine's idea, outlined in the second part of *The Rights of Man*, 1792, and in *Agrarian Justice*, 1797, that a property tax could be used as a means of furnishing a range of social welfare payments. For Spence this was merely the thief returning to his victims a part of what had been stolen. On Paine's plans see, for example, M. Philp, *Paine*, Oxford: Oxford University Press, 1989, 84–93. For Spence's attack on them, see, in particular, *The Rights of Infants*.
36. T. Spence, *Description of Spensonia*, London: 1795, *PWS*, 32.
37. T. Spence, *A Fragment of an Ancient Prophecy*, London: 1796, *PWS*, 45; Spence, *The Restorer of Society*, 71; T. Spence, *The Reign of Felicity*, London: 1796, *PWS*, 44.
38. T. Spence, *A Letter from Ralph Hodge*, London: 1795, *PWS*, 21; Spence, *The End of Oppression*, 37.
39. Spence, *A Letter from Ralph Hodge*, 21, 25.
40. Spence, *The Real Rights of Man*, 3.
41. Spence, *The Rights of Infants*, 52; T. Spence, *The Constitution of a Perfect Commonwealth*, London: 1798, *PWS*, 61.
42. Spence, *The Restorer of Society*, 75.
43. Spence, *The Real Rights of Man*, 3.
44. Ibid.
45. Spence, *The Restorer of Society*, 87.

46. Knox, 'Thomas Spence', 98; H.T. Dickinson, *Liberty and Property, Political Ideology in Eighteenth Century Britain*, London: Methuen, 1977, 267.
47. T. Spence, *A Supplement to the History of Robinson Crusoe*, London: 1782, *PWS*, 7.
48. T. Spence, *A Dream*, London: 1807[?], *PWE*, 119.
49. Spence, *A Supplement*, 15.
50. Spence, *The Reign of Felicity*, 44.
51. Spence, *A Dream*, 19; T. Spence, *Spence's Recantation of the End of Oppression*, London: 1795, *PWE*, 39; *Description of Spensonia*, 33.
52. Ibid., 26.
53. Ashraf, *The Life and Times of Thomas Spence*, 121.
54. Dickinson, *Liberty and Property*, 268.
55. He was to leave the LCS as a result of its defence of private property, Ashraf, *The Life and Times of Thomas Spence*, 72.
56. Spence died on 1 September 1814.
57. O. Rudkin, *Thomas Spence and his Connections*, New York: Kelley, 1966, 139; ibid., 141; T. Malthus, *Essay on Population*, 5th edn., London: 1817, 273–4, 'an idea has lately prevailed amongst the lower classes of society that the land is the people's farm the rent of which must be equally divided amongst them'.
58. Anon., *An Inquiry into those Principles Respecting the Nature of Demand and the Necessity of Consumption*, London: 1815, 108.
59. As regards the impact of Spence's thought one might also note that two biographical sketches of him were published within two decades of his death: T. Evans, *A Brief Sketch of the Life of Mr. Thomas Spence*, London: 1821; A. Davenport, *The Life, Writings and Principles of Thomas Spence*, London: 1836.
60. See below, Chapter 9.
61. G.D.H. Cole, *A History of Socialist Thought*, Vol. 1, *Socialist Thought: the Forerunners*, London: Macmillan, 1959, 25; M. Chase, *The People's Farm, English Agrarian Radicalism, 1775–1840*, Oxford: Oxford University Press, 1988, 18.
62. Further, the idea of the state asserting some measure of control over the nation's primary productive resource and using it for the benefit of all finds expression in works such as William Hodgson's *Commonwealth of Reason*, London: 1795 and James Parkinson's *Revolution without Bloodshed*, London: 1794; the former suggesting the nationalisation of uncultivated church lands for the settlement of the poor together with national manufactories and old age pensions, while the latter advocated a social reform programme which implied a significant measure of national control over the economy.
63. See Rudkin, *Thomas Spence and his Connections*, 17n.
64. W. Ogilvie, *An Essay on the Right of Property in Land* [1782], in M. Beer, *Pioneers of Land Reform*, London: Bell, 1920, 35, 39. The major intellectual influences on Ogilvie were those of the

Scottish Enlightenment philosophers – David Hume, Adam
Ferguson and Adam Smith. For an excellect discussion of
Ogilvie's work and those who helped shape his thought, see
Stafford, *Socialism Radicalism and Nostalgia*, 107–20.
65. Ogilvie, *An Essay*, 41, 40.
66. Ibid., 43.
67. Ibid., 44.
68. Ibid., 92. Like Spence, Ogilvie's views here owe something to
his understanding of the Mosaic law outlined in chapter 25 of
Leviticus, but also to the agrarian laws applied in the Roman
Republic under the Gracchi.
69. Ibid., 165.
70. Ibid., 85.
71. Ibid., 152, 171n.
72. Ibid., 59, 56n.
73. Ibid., 69, 52n, 53n.
74. Ibid., 89.
75. Ibid., 50.
76. Ibid., 49.
77. Ibid., 50.
78. Ibid.
79. Ibid., 53.

Chapter 2

1. W. Cobbett, *Observations on the Emigration of Dr. Priestley*,
Philadelphia: 1794, in N. Thompson and D. Eastwood (eds),
The Collected Social and Political Writings of William Cobbett, 16
vols, London: Routledge/Thoemmes, 1998, 1, 17, hereafter
CWC.
2. W. Cobbett, *The Rush-light, a Peep into a Republican Court of
Justice*, New York: 1800, *CWC*, 1, 194, my emphasis.
3. W. Cobbett, 'Note on Priestley's charity sermon for poor
emigrants', 1801, *CWC*, 1, 210–11, my emphasis. This was
originally published in Cobbett's paper the *Porcupine*.
4. P. Deane, 'War and industrialisation' in J. Winter (ed.), *War
and Economic Development: Essays in Memory of David Joslin*,
Cambridge: Cambridge University Press, 1975, 93.
5. Mitchell, *British Historical Statistics*, 587.
6. The other 19 per cent was accounted for by land and assessed
taxes and the income tax, introduced by Pitt in 1799.
7. Mitchell, *British Historical Statistics*, 601.
8. See P. Harling, *The Waning of 'Old Corruption', the Politics of
Economical Reform in Britain, 1779–1846*, Oxford: Clarendon,
1996, 72.
9. G. Heuckel, 'English farming profits during the Napoleonic
Wars, 1793–1815', *Explorations in Economic History*, 13, 1976,
343; Harling, *The Waning of 'Old Corruption'*, 69.

10. Mitchell, *British Historical Statistics*, 721; J. Mokyr and N. Savin, 'Stagflation in historical perspective: the Napoleonic Wars revisited', *Research in Economic History*, 1, 1976, 199.
11. Heuckel, 'English farming profits', 343.
12. F.M.L. Thompson, *English Landed Society in the Nineteenth Century*, London: Routledge and Kegan Paul, 1963, 215.
13. W. Cobbett, 'Prospects of war: to Lord Hawkesbury', *Political Register*, March 1803, *CWC*, 3, 289.
14. W. Cobbett, 'Pitt system', *Political Register*, July 1802, *CWC*, 3, 261.
15. W. Cobbett, 'Stock jobbing nation', *Political Register*, May 1803, *CWC*, 3, 293.
16. W. Cobbett, *Cobbett's Manchester Lectures in Support of Fourteen Reform Propositions*, London: 1832, *CWC*, 11, 95.
17. T. Paine, *The Decline of the English System of Finance*, London: 1796, 11.
18. W. Cobbett, 'To the journeymen and labourers', *Political Register*, November 1816, *CWC*, 8, 2.
19. Ibid., 3.
20. W. Cobbett, 'A letter to the Luddites', *Political Register*, November, 1816, *CWC*, 8, 25.
21. W. Cobbett, 'Second letter to Lord Grey' *Political Register*, Vol. 37, No. 23, 1820, col. 1568.
22. 'Petition approved at the general meeting of reformers of Newcastle', *Northern Reformers' Monthly Magazine*, 1, No. 4, 1823, 136.
23. Cobbett, 'To the journeymen and labourers', 9.
24. Ibid., 4.
25. Cobbett, 'A letter to the Luddites', 19, 27.
26. Cobbett, 'To the journeymen and labourers', 3.
27. Harling, *The Waning of Old Corruption*, 138.
28. Mitchell, *British Historical Statistics*, 587.
29. Harling, *The Waning of Old Corruption*, 20.
30. Ibid., 21.
31. W. Cobbett, 'Perish commerce!', *Political Register*, November/December 1807, *CWC*, 4, 346; 380.
32. Ibid., 375, 374.

Chapter 3

1. C. Behagg, *Politics and Production in the Early Nineteenth Century*, London: Routledge, 1990, 2.
2. 'Because mechanisation and factory concentration were absent, this did not mean that the larger capitalist concerns did not increase the competitive tempo at all levels', P. Joyce, 'Work', in F.M.L. Thompson (ed.), *The Cambridge Social History of Britain, People and Their Environment*, Cambridge: Cambridge University Press, 1990, Vol. 2, 155.

3. Ibid.
4. Though the assault upon the practice of a moral economy had begun long before. Thus A.J. Randall has discussed the case of the Gloucestershire weavers who, in 1756, struck successfully to secure an Act for the determination of wages after employers had moved to cut piece rates, only to see that Act repealed one year later in 1757 after a campaign by employers which rested on *laissez-faire* principles. See A. Randall, 'The industrial moral economy of the Gloucestershire weavers', in J. Rule (ed.), *British Trade Unionism, 1750–1850, the Formative Years*, London: Longman, 1988.
5. J. Rule, 'The formative years of British trade unionism: an overview', in ibid., 10.
6. J. Rule, *The Labouring Classes in Early Industrial England, 1750–1850*, London: Longman, 1986, 108.
7. M. Berg, *The Age of Manufactures, 1700–1820, Industry, Innovation and Work in Britain*, 2nd edn, London: Routledge, 1994, 198–9.
8. Ibid., 203–5.
9. W. Hoskins, *The Midland Peasant: the Economic and Social History of a Leicestershire Village*, London: Macmillan, 1965, 269.
10. On this see Charlesworth, 'The development of the English rural proletariat', 62; and Reed, 'Class and conflict', 8.
11. On this see, for example, J. Brewer, N. McKendrick and J.H. Plumb, *The Birth of a Consumer Society, the Commercialization of Eighteenth Century England*, Europa: 1982, 206.
12. Mitchell, *British Historical Statistics*, 722.
13. Behagg, *Politics and Production*, 7.
14. Joyce, 'Work', 177, 163.

Chapter 4

1. The latter clauses by legislating for a seven-year apprenticeship gave trades a measure of control over the flow of labour into an occupation.
2. For example, the use of half-pay apprentices by Macclesfield silk manufacturers and Coventry ribbon makers in the post-1815 period.
3. For a discussion of the repeal of these acts, see J.H. Clapham, 'The Spitalfields Acts, 1773–1824', *Economic Journal*, 26, 1916, 459–71.
4. *First and Second Reports from the Select Committee on the Petitions of Ribbon Weavers with Minutes of Evidence*, British parliamentary papers, 1818, Shannon: Irish University Press, 1968, 2.
5. G. Henson, *A History of the Framework Knitters*, Leicester: 1831, 1, 232–3.
6. *Committee on the Petitions of Ribbon Weavers*, 52.

7. R. Hall, *An Appeal to the Public on the Subject of the Framework Knitters' Fund*, London: 1820, 6; W. Jackson, *An Appeal to the Framework Knitters of the Town and County of Leicester*, Leicester: 1833, 6.
8. Hall, *An Appeal*, 7.
9. Anon., *A Petition from the Journeymen Broad Silk Weavers of Spitalfields and its vicinity*, London: 1828, 7.
10. A. Smith, *An Inquiry into the Nature and Causes of the Wealth of Nations*, 2 vols, Oxford: Oxford University Press, 1976, 1, 84.
11. Hall, *An Appeal*, 6.
12. Anon., *A Petition*, 3.
13. Henson, *A History of the Framework Knitters*, 1, 234.
14. W. Jackson, *An Address to the Framework-Knitters of the Town and County of Leicester*, Leicester: 1833, 4.
15. Writers such as Jane Marcet, Harriet Martineau and Charles Knight.
16. J. Ovington, *A Certain Remedy for Existing Distresses or, the Labouring Man's Advocate*, London: 1816, 41; R. Hall, *A Reply to the Principal Objections Advanced by Cobbett and Others against The Framework Knitters' Friendly Relief Society*, Leicester: 1821, 6; W. Hale, *An Appeal to the Public in Defence of the Spitalfields Acts*, London: 1822, 16; ibid., 29; 'Petition of the silk weavers of Macclesfield', 1817, quoted from *Committee on the Petitions of Ribbon Weavers*, 89, my emphasis throughout.
17. A. Larcher, *The Good and Bad Effects of High and Low Wages*, London: 1823, 9; ibid., 13, my emphasis throughout.
18. Henson, *A History of the Framework Knitters*, 1, 234.
19. 'Declaration of silk manufacturers', 1818, quoted from *Committee on the Petitions of Ribbon Weavers*, 196–7.
20. Anon., *A Petition*, 4.
21. *Committee on the Petitions of Ribbon Weavers*, 179–80.
22. Hall, *An Appeal*, 8.
23. Ovington, *A Certain Remedy*, 74.
24. Anon., *A Petition*, 5.
25. Anon., *A Letter Addressed to the Members of Both Houses of Parliament on the Distresses of the Handloom Weavers*, Bolton: 1834, 6; J. Maxwell, *Manual Labour versus Machinery*, London: 1834, 10–11.
26. Hall, *A Reply*, 6; Hall, *An Appeal*, 8.
27. Jackson, *An address*, 8.
28. M. Huberman, *Escape from the Market, Negotiating Work in Lancashire*, Cambridge: Cambridge University Press, 1996.
29. As Claeys has put it, 'for much of the nineteenth century political economy successfully dictated the terms of debate about such vital issues as the poor laws, trades' unions, hours and conditions of labour, emigration, the morals of the poor and the extension of the factory system', *Citizens and Saints, Politics and Anti-politics in Early British Socialism*, 1989, Cambridge: Cambridge University Press, 1989, 144.

Chapter 5

1. It was Francis Place, for example, who introduced him to Ricardo's *On the Principles of Political Economy and Taxation*, London: 1817.
2. T. Hodgskin, *Travels in the North of Germany Describing the Present State of the Social and Political Institutions*, 2 vols, Edinburgh: 1820, 2, 204; 1, 360.
3. In particular the *laissez-faire* reading of Smith furnished by the Scottish philosopher, Dugald Stewart.
4. 'Paley's *Moral Philosophy* was one of the most frequently cited sources throughout Hodgskin's career', D. Stack, *Nature and Artifice: the Life and Thought of Thomas Hodgskin, 1787–1869*, London: Royal Historical Society, Boydell and Brewer, 1998, 96.
5. Given the early intellectual influences upon him – Adam Smith, James Mill, David Ricardo, T.R. Malthus – this is not surprising.
6. D. Ricardo, *On the Principles of Political Economy and Taxation*, P. Sraffa (ed.), *The Works and Correspondence of David Ricardo*, Vol. 1, Cambridge: Cambridge University Press, 1981, 5.
7. T. Hodgskin, *Labour Defended against the Claims of Capital*, London: 1825, 83.
8. Ibid., 30.
9. Ibid., 67n.
10. Ibid., 31.
11. See T. Hodgskin, *Popular Political Economy, Four Lectures Delivered at the London Mechanics' Institution*, London: 1827, 219; also ibid., 185.
12. Hodgskin, *Labour Defended*, 44.
13. Ibid., 63, 71.
14. Ibid., 70, my emphasis; Hodgskin, *Popular Political Economy*, 248.
15. J. Lalor, *Money and Morals*, London: 1852, xxiv.
16. Hodgskin, *Labour Defended*, 27.
17. G. Stedman Jones, 'Rethinking Chartism', in *Languages of Class, Studies in English Working-class History, 1832–1982*, Cambridge: Cambridge University Press, 1983, 134.
18. *Labour Defended*, 70.
19. Cf. Stack, *Nature and Artifice*, 131, 'Hodgskin did not therefore go beyond traditional radicalism ... Class antagonism inhered in extra-economic relations.' But see also Stack's ambivalence – 'By focusing on fixed capital and stressing the antagonism of labourers to capitalists Hodgskin moved radicalism beyond merely agrarian concerns, and suggested a transcendence of traditional radicalism', ibid., 135.
20. Hodgskin, *Labour Defended*, 75, my emphasis.
21. Ibid., 78.
22. Joyce, 'Work', 167; Stedman Jones, 'Rethinking Chartism', 134, 137.

23. Stack, *Nature and Artifice*, 131, 208, my emphasis.
24. Hodgskin, *Labour Defended*, 71.
25. Ibid., 88–9.
26. Ibid., 88.
27. Note here I. Prothero's pertinent and telling remark that 'many of Hodgskin's ideas did correspond with those of the London artisans ... Active employers were workers, though too highly paid, but as providers of capital had interests opposed to the men', *Artisans and Politics, the Life and Times of John Gast*, Folkestone: Dawson, 1979, 208.
28. Hodgskin, *Labour Defended*, 103, 92.
29. Ibid., 104.
30. Stedman Jones, 'Rethinking Chartism', 135, 136, 137.
31. Hodgskin, *Popular Political Economy*, 261.
32. Ibid., 199; T. Hodgskin, *The Natural and Artificial Rights of Property Contrasted*, London: 1832, 49.
33. Ibid., 98.
34. Ibid., 149.
35. Ibid., 53, my emphasis.
36. Ibid., my emphasis.
37. Ibid., 12, 15.
38. Quoted from A. Bain, *James Mill, a Biography*, London: Longman, 1882, 63–4; C. Knight, *The Rights of Industry*, London: 1831, 16. It is interesting to note as Stack has pointed out, *Nature and Artifice*, 146–7, that 'it was precisely the same group of economists who noticed the force of Hodgskin's assault upon capital who were foremost in developing alternative justifications like the "abstinence theory of profit"', i.e. writers such as G.P. Scrope, Samuel Read and Mountifort Longfield.
39. Though *The Natural and Artificial Rights* was published in 1832 it had been written in 1829.
40. Hodgskin wrote numerous articles for the *Economist* between 1843 and 1857 and articles and editorials for the *Brighton Guardian* between 1855 and 1869.
41. K. Marx, *Theories of Surplus Value*, 3 vols, London: Lawrence and Wishart, 1972, 3, 297.

Chapter 6

1. The influence of Enlightenment philosophers such as Helvetius and Rousseau was important here.
2. R. Owen, *The Life of Robert Owen Written by Himself*, 2 vols, London: 1857–58, 1A, 64.
3. 'The immediate cause of the present distress is the depreciation of human labour. This has been occasioned by the general introduction of mechanism into the manufactures of Europe', R. Owen, 'Report to the committee for the relief of the manufacturing poor', 1817, *Life*, 1A, 86.

4. R. Owen, 'Two memorials on behalf of the working classes', 1818, *Life*, 1A, 220; R. Owen, 'A catechism of the new view of society and three addresses', in A.L. Morton, *The Life and Ideas of Robert Owen*, London: Lawrence and Wishart, 1962, 181.

5. R. Owen, *A New View of Society, Essays on the Formation of Human Character* [1816], ed. V.A.C. Gattrell, Harmondsworth: Pelican, 1970, 66.

6. R. Owen, *Report to the County of Lanark of a Plan for Relieving Public Distress* [1821], London: Dent, 1927, 248.

7. 'This change in the standard of value would immediately open the most advantageous domestic markets ... nor while this standard continued could evil arise in future from want of markets', ibid., 251.

8. Ibid.

9. R. Owen, *The Address of the Working Classes of Devonshire*, Exeter: 1830, 1.

10. F. Engels, *The Condition of the Working Class in England*, St Albans: Panther, 1974, 262.

11. Owen, *A New View of Society*, 76.

12. Owen, *Life*, 1, 73.

13. R. Owen, *An Explanation of the Causes of Distress*, London: 1823, 5.

14. Owen, *Life*, 1, 20.

15. R. Owen, *An Address to the Operative Manufacturing and Agricultural Labourers*, London: 1830, 1.

16. Owen, 'Two memorials', 228.

17. R. Owen, 'An address to British manufacturers', 1818, *Life* 1A, 85.

18. R. Owen, *Development of the Plan for the Relief of the Poor*, London: 1820, 4.

19. Owen, 'Two memorials', 230.

20. W. Thompson, *An Inquiry into the Principles of the Distribution of Wealth most Conducive to Human Happiness*, London: 1824, x.

21. It has been suggested that George Mudie, an early co-operator and editor of the *Economist*, 1821–22, the first major Owenite journal, may also have been an important influence on Thompson. See G. Claeys, *Machinery, Money and the Millennium, from Moral Economy to Socialism, 1815–60*, Cambridge: Polity, 1987, 68.

22. G.J. Holyoake, *A History of Co-operation*, London: Unwin, 1906, 14.

23. Thompson, *Inquiry*, 7.

24. Ibid., 363.

25. Ibid., 224, 225.

26. In *Citizens and Saints*, 25, Claeys has detailed two different conceptions of politics emerging within socialism from the mid-1820s. 'One of these remained more traditionally constitutional and political, while attempting to extend the scope of democ-

ratic participation. The other, more utopian, anti-political and indebted to religiously inspired perfectionism sought to transcend government as it was understood generally.' Thompson was certainly a progenitor of the former strain of socialist thinking; one which Claeys has denominated 'social radicalism'.

27. Thompson, *Inquiry*, 241.
28. Ibid.
29. Ibid., 171.
30. Ibid., 172.
31. Ibid., 171.
32. Ibid., 423, 241.
33. Ibid., 587.
34. Ibid., 590.
35. Ibid., 246.
36. Ibid., 150.
37. Ibid., 97.
38. Ibid., 193, 504.
39. Ibid., 225, 552.
40. W. Thompson, *Labor Rewarded, the Claims of Labor and Capital Conciliated, by One of the Idle Classes*, London: 1827, 18.
41. Ibid., 11, 53.
42. Ibid., 5.
43. Ibid., 15.
44. Ibid., 36.
45. Ibid., 14, 41, 44, my emphasis.
46. Ibid., 96.
47. Ibid., 63, my emphasis.
48. Ibid., 23.
49. Ibid., 55.
50. Ibid., 7.
51. Ibid., 8, 86.
52. Ibid., 119.
53. Ibid., 115.
54. Ibid., 106–7.
55. Ibid., 108–9.
56. Ibid., 106–7.
57. Ibid., 116, my emphasis.
58. Ibid., 16.
59. For a discussion of Mudie's political economy and his activities in the co-operative movement, see Claeys, *Machinery, Money and the Millennium*, 67–89.
60. For an account of Owenite and other co-operative communities in Britain and America, see R.G. Garnett, *Co-operation and the Owenite Socialist Communities in Britain, 1825–45*, Manchester: Manchester University Press, 1972; and J.F.C. Harrison, *Owen and the Owenites in Britain and America, the Quest for the New Moral World*, London: Routledge, 1969.
61. Garnett, *Co-operation and the Owenite Socialist Communities*, 51.

62. Harrison, *Owen and the Owenites*, 202.
63. The first by Benjamin Warden and the second by William King.
64. On this see W.H. Oliver, 'The labour exchange phase of the co-operative movement', *Oxford Economic Papers*, 10, 1958, 355–67.
65. E.P. Thompson, *The Making of the English Working Class*, Harmondsworth: Penguin, 1975, 882–3.
66. *New Moral World*, 20 February 1836, 130; Thompson, *Inquiry*, 193.
67. For a discussion of the membership of communities, see Harrison, *Owen and the Owenites*, 184ff.
68. It has been estimated that in 1815 no less than 925,000, or 8.5 per cent of the population were members of friendly societies. See Garnett, *Co-operation and the Owenite Socialist Communities*, 11.
69. Harrison, *Owen and the Owenites*, 197. Andrew Larcher, *A Remedy for Establishing Universal Peace*, London: 1795, proposed a co-operative community and trading society for Spitalfields silk weavers.
70. On this see Claeys, *Citizens and Saints*, 58.
71. Owen, *Report to the County of Lanark*, 259, my emphasis.
72. Harrison, *Owen and the Owenites*, 56.
73. Thompson, *Making*, 883.
74. M. Hennell, *An Outline of the Various Social Systems and Communities*, London: 1844, lxxxi; *Inquiry*, 521–2; ibid., 65; R. Owen, *Observations on the Effect of the Manufacturing System* [1815], London: Dent, 1927, 122.

Chapter 7

1. On this see Behagg, *Politics and Production*, 6–9; and Berg, *The Age of Manufactures*, 205.
2. For a discussion of the range of trades involved in the GNCTU, see W. Oliver, 'The Consolidated Trades' Union of 1834', *Economic History Review*, 17, 1965, 85.
3. R. Sykes, 'Trade unionism and class consciousness: the "revolutionary" period of general unionism, 1829–34', in Rule, *British Trade Unionism*, 185; on this point see also Oliver, 'The Grand Consolidated Trades' Union of 1834', 78, 80.
4. R. Postgate, *The Builders' History*, London: The National Federation of Building Trade Operatives, 1923, 57.
5. M. Haynes, 'Class and class conflict in the early nineteenth century: Northampton shoemakers and the Grand National Consolidated Trades' Union', *Literature and History*, 5, 1977, 80.
6. Sykes, 'Trade unionism and class consciousness', 186.
7. Prothero, *Artisans and Politics*, 301.
8. Rule, *The Labouring Classes in the Eighteenth Century*, 296.
9. Postgate, *The Builders' History*, 112.

10. R. Fryson, 'Unionism, class and community in the 1830s: aspects of the National Union of Operative Potters' in Rule, *British Trade Unionism*, 204.
11. Sykes, 'Trade unionism and class consciousness', 186.
12. T. Parsinnen and I. Prothero, 'The London tailors' strike of 1834 and the collapse of the Grand National Consolidated Trades' Union, a police spy's report', *International Review of Social History*, 22, 1977, 72, 77.
13. James Morrison was editor of the *Pioneer*, 1833–34; J.E. 'Shepherd' Smith was editor of the *Crisis* from 1832–34. For descriptions of these and other working-class papers of the early 1830s, see J. Wiener, *A Descriptive Find List of Unstamped British Periodicals, 1830–36*, London: The Bibliographical Society, 1970.
14. For estimates of the growth of early nineteenth century fixed capital investment in manufacturing and mining, see C.H. Feinstein and S. Pollard (eds), *Studies in Capital Formation in the United Kingdom, 1750–1920*, Oxford: Clarendon, 1988, 429, 444.
15. R. Harrison, G. Woolven and R. Duncan, *The Warwick Guide to British Labour Periodicals, 1790–1970: a Checklist*, Hassocks: Harvester, 1977, 414.
16. A strong case for the author being James Morrison has been made in an unpublished monograph by J. Sever, *James Morrison of the Pioneer*, 1963.
17. 'Senex', 'On associated labour II', *Pioneer*, 22 March 1834, 258.
18. 'Senex', 'On associated labour III', *Pioneer*, 5 April 1834, 282.
19. 'Senex', 'On associated labour XII', *Pioneer*, 14 June 1834, 403.
20. 'Senex', 'On associated labour XIV', *Pioneer*, 28 June 1834, 418; 'Senex', 'On associated labour IV', *Pioneer*, 12 April 1834, 290.
21. L.R. 'Change of government', *Pioneer*, 15 February 1834, 202.
22. Concord, 'To Thomas Attwood', *Pioneer*, 5 October 1833, 34.
23. Anon., 'To the productive classes', *Pioneer*, 14 September 1833, 15.
24. Editorial, 'Universal suffrage', *Pioneer*, 31 May 1834, 377.
25. 'Senex', 'On associated labour VII', *Pioneer*, 10 May 1834, 339.
26. 'Concord', 'To the master builders of England', *Pioneer*, 28 September 1833, 26, my emphasis.
27. Editorial, *Pioneer*, 22 March 1834, 257.
28. Anon., 'To the operative builders', *Pioneer*, 14 September 1834, 11.
29. 'Concord', 'To the operatives', *Pioneer*, 12 October 1833, 42; *Pioneer*, 25 January, 1834, 165; Editorial, *Pioneer*, 3 May 1834, 329.
30. Anon., 'Address to unionists', *Pioneer*, 7 June 1834, 399.
31. Anon, 'On society', *Pioneer*, 7 September 1833, 6; 'Concord', 'To the operative builders', ibid., 2.
32. Editorial, *Pioneer*, 10 May 1834, 337.

33. 'Senex', 'On associated labour IX', *Pioneer*, 24 May 1834, 363; 'Senex', 'On associated labour VIII', *Pioneer*, 17 May 1834, 354.
34. J. Mitchell, 'To the Central Committee of London', *Pioneer*, 10 May 1834, 347.
35. 'Concord', 'To Thomas Attwood', 34; 'Senex', 'On associated labour III', 282.
36. 'Concord', 'To the operative classes', *Pioneer*, 30 November 1833, 98.
37. Anon., 'To the United Lodges of builders in Leamington', *Pioneer*, 23 November 1833, 89; Editorial, *Pioneer*, 10 May 1834, 337.
38. 'Concord', 'To the operative builders', *Pioneer*, 7 September 1833, 3.
39. 'Senex', 'Letters on associated labour XII', 401.
40. Editorial, *Pioneer*, 28 December 1833, 129.
41. Editorial, *Pioneer*, 31 May 1834, 377–8.
42. 'Concord', 'To the master builders of England', 26.
43. Even the General Union or, as it would become, a House of Trades was seen by some as doing little more than confirming the decisions of the 'districts' – here the emphasis was very much on the decentralisation of the power of economic decision-making. 'A trading or labouring community can only be governed or legislated for by men intimately acquainted with the minutest interests of labour; and, indeed, little would be left for the supreme government to decide upon, beyond confirming the decisions of the districts', ibid.
44. L.R., 'Change of government', *Pioneer*, 15 February 1834, 202.
45. Anon., 'A dialogue on society', *Pioneer*, 14 September 1833, 14.

Chapter 8

1. J. Gray, *The Social System, a Treatise on the Principle of Exchange*, Edinburgh: 1831, 339–40. Much of the autobiographical material we have on Gray comes from the Appendix to this work.
2. A view given statistical substance by detailed reference to Patrick Colquhoun's, *Treatise on the Population, Wealth, Power and Resources of the British Empire*, London: 1814.
3. J. Gray, *A Lecture on Human Happiness*, London: 1825, 3.
4. It is difficult to reconcile this with Claeys' view that 'the mode of exchange [was] ... not of central concern in the *Lecture*'. See Claeys, *Machinery, Money and the Millennium*, 121.
5. Gray, *A Lecture*, 47.
6. Ibid., 53.
7. This preoccupation with co-operative communities led Gray to take an interest in that established by Abram Combe and Archibald Hamilton at Orbiston near Motherwell in 1825.

However, when he visited it in that year his reaction, as expressed in *A Word of Advice to the Orbistonians*, 1826, was highly critical.

8. Gray, *The Social System*, 57.
9. Ibid., 236.
10. Ibid., 66, 275.
11. Ibid., 60.
12. Ibid., 57. That said, Gray wrote in *The Social System* that parliamentary reform might expedite what he referred to as 'greater reformations'. But he was also quick to add that 'these are but the steps to improvement; they are but processes in the manufacture of the material of that garment in which society will yet be splendidly arrayed', ibid., 170.
13. Ibid., 90.
14. As regards the idea of economic planning it should be noted that George Mudie was an important precursor of Gray and Bray. See Claeys, *Machinery, Money and the Millennium*, 75.
15. Gray, *The Social System*, vii–viii. In the *Lecture*, 41, Gray wrote, 'Things have been finding their level ever since the creation: when, we ask, is that level to be found? It is very clear that at least five hundred thousand Irish have been nearly finding their level, and it appears to us that the level they have found is the level we all deserve to find, if we do not alter our mode of acting.'
16. *The Social System*, 38.
17. Ibid., 331.
18. Ibid., 32.
19. Ibid., 108–9.
20. Ibid., 333.
21. Ibid., 31.
22. Ibid., 323.
23. Ibid., 31, 32.
24. Ibid., 88.
25. Ibid., 325.
26. Ibid., 292.
27. Ibid., 45.
28. Ibid., 34.
29. Ibid., 104.
30. Ibid., 105.
31. Ibid., 149.
32. Ibid., 16.
33. Ibid., 64.
34. Ibid., 100.
35. Ibid., 66.
36. See below.
37. Ibid., ix.
38. Ibid., 25.
39. K. Marx, *The Poverty of Philosophy*, Moscow: Progress, 1976, 190, my emphasis.

40. J. Gray, *An Efficient Remedy for the Distress of Nations*, Edinburgh: 1842, 5.
41. *Labour's Wrongs* was indifferently reviewed and shortly after its publication Bray returned to the United States, in May 1842, though not before drafting *A Voyage from Utopia* (1841–42) as a riposte to those who had categorised the prescriptions of the former work as 'impracticable' and 'visionary'. During the rest of his life in the United States Bray combined the careers of journalism and farming. Throughout the 1860s and 1870s he contributed short articles and letters on socialism and labour questions to a wide variety of American papers. These included, amongst others, the *Irish World*, the *Denver Labour Inquirer*, the *Hartford Examiner*, *John Swinton's Paper*, the *Detroit Socialist*, the *Spectator*, the *Chicago and Cincinnati Socialist* and the *Milwaukee Emancipator*. In the 1870s and 1880s he was active in the American labour movement and, in May 1886, was initiated into the syndicalist Knights of Labor. He also wrote several pamphlets for the Detroit Socialist Tract Association.
42. J.F. Bray, *Labour's Wrongs and Labour's Remedy, or the Age of Might and the Age of Right*, Leeds: 1839, 15.
43. Ibid., 17.
44. Ibid., 67.
45. Ibid., 61–2.
46. Ibid., 93.
47. Ibid., 99.
48. Ibid., 17, my emphasis.
49. Ibid., 106.
50. Ibid., 17.
51. Ibid., 48.
52. Ibid., 50.
53. Ibid., 49.
54. Ibid., 48.
55. Ibid., 75.
56. Ibid., 52.
57. Ibid., 61.
58. Ibid., 60, my emphasis.
59. Ibid., 77, 98, my emphasis.
60. Ibid., 171, 169–70.
61. Ibid., 171.
62. Ibid., 44.
63. Ibid., 164, 163.
64. Among other things this would include the servicing and liquidation of the government stock issued to purchase the capital in the first place.
65. Ibid., 170.
66. Ibid., 160.
67. Ibid.
68. Ibid., 162.

69. Ibid., 162, 181.
70. Ibid., 194.
71. Ibid., 157, 180.
72. Ibid., 18.
73. Ibid., 161–2.
74. Ibid., 158.
75. Ibid., 194.

Chapter 9

1. James 'Bronterre' O'Brien, 1804–64, the son of an Irish wine
merchant, came to England in 1830 to train as a lawyer but
soon became embroiled in the movement for radical political
reform. In the early 1830s he was also involved in the struggle
for an unstamped working-class press, editing the *Midland
Representative* and, most famously, the *Poor Man's Guardian*.
Inspired in his political thinking by the French Revolution, he
translated Buonarotti's *History of Babeuf's Conspiracy for
Equality*, 1836, and produced the first volume of an adulatory
Life and Character of Maximilien Robespierre in 1838. In the
period after 1838 he played a prominent role in the Chartist
movement, editing papers such as the *Operative*, the *Southern
Star*, the *National Reformer and Manx Weekly Review* and, for
these efforts, acquired the sobriquet of the 'schoolmaster of
Chartism'. O'Brien also led one of the two most important
groups which emerged after the failure of the third Chartist
petition in 1848 – the National Reform League. His one major
theoretical work, *The Rise, Progress and Phases of Human Slavery*
was published in 1855, though the first chapter saw the light of
day in *Reynold's Political Instructor* in 1849. Parts of the work
were also to be republished in the 1880s, one as a pamphlet
entitled *State Socialism*, London: 1885.

Like O'Brien, whom he referred to as a 'guide, philosopher
and friend', George Julian Harney (1817–97) became involved
in radical politics in the 1830s and, in particular, the fight
against the newspaper tax. He played an important role during
the period of Chartism, helping to found the London
Democratic Association in opposition to the less radical
London Workingmen's Association and acted as a connecting
link between British Chartists and European republicans and
socialists. He helped establish the Society of Fraternal
Democrats in 1846 with the objective of bringing together
Chartists with foreign exiles in London, amongst them, Karl
Marx. In the late 1840s and early 1850s he successively edited
the *Democratic Review*, the *Red Republican* and the *Friend of the
People* which gave considerable space to continental thinkers
and continental politics.

Ernest Jones (1816–69) joined the Chartist movement in 1845. He was convicted for insurrectionary agitation in 1848 and spent two years in prison. His most important theoretical writing is contained in his *Notes to the People*, a periodical published in the period 1851–52. Like Harney, Jones was friendly for a time with Marx and Engels, though G.D.H. Cole's view that 'the socialism of Ernest Jones, as it developed after 1848, was in its essentials that of Marx' is well wide of the mark. However, so too, but in a very different way, is Max Beer's assessment of his 'political and social writings' as of 'no importance'. See Cole, *Socialist Thought*, 151 and M. Beer, *A History of British Socialism*, Vol. 2, London: Bell, 1929, 159. On the contrary, Jones' analysis of mid-century British capitalism displays considerable critical insight; not least in his discussion of the causes and consequences of the concentration of ownership and industrial power. After 1848 it was Jones and Harney who reorganised and led the National Charter Association. In Jones' *Notes*, as in the periodicals of Harney, there is also a marked interest in continental politics.

2. Trades union activity was stirred by events such as the engineering employers' lockout of early 1852 and the lockout of Preston textile workers in late 1853.

3. There were those who before this had 'sought to unite Chartist and Owenite convictions in a single programme', in particular, James Napier Bailey, who 'aimed to fuse the identity of Socialism with that of Republican democracy', see Claeys, *Citizens and Saints*, 209, 235.

4. E. Jones, 'An address to the people', in J. Saville, *Ernest Jones: Chartist*, London: Lawrence and Wishart, 1952, 111.

5. 'Programme adopted by the Chartist Convention of 1851' in ibid., 258.

6. A.R. Schoyen, *The Chartist Challenge: a Portrait of George Julian Harney*, London: Heinemann, 1958, 177.

7. G.J. Harney, 'To the working classes', *Democratic Review*, 1, 1849, 205.

8. H. Morton, 'The red flag in 1850', *Red Republican*, 13 July 1850, 26.

9. E. Jones, 'The young republic and the rights of labour', *Notes to the People*, 1, 1851, 276.

10. G.J. Harney, 'The Charter and something more', *Red Republican*, 22 June 1850, 2.

11. E. Jones, 'Trades' grievances', ibid., 1, 1851, 422.

12. E. Jones, 'Trades' grievances', ibid., 2, 1852, 783.

13. E. Jones, 'The iron trades', ibid., 2, 1852, 976.

14. E. Jones, 'The co-operative movement', ibid., 1, 1851, 473.

15. E. Jones, 'Discussion at Halifax', ibid., 2, 1852, 797.

16. Jones, 'The co-operative movement', 473.

17. 'June 29, 1848' by Dr. Marx, ibid., 1, 1851, 312–14; The *Manifesto* appeared in the *Red Republican* of 9, 16, 23 and 30 November 1850.

18. See, for example, F.E., 'The ten hours question', *Democratic Review*, 1, 1850, 373.

19. A.J.P. Taylor (ed.), K. Marx and F. Engels, *The Communist Manifesto*, 1848, Harmondsworth: Penguin, 1967, 104.

20. In the *Democratic Review* of January and April 1850.

21. Schoyen, *The Chartist Challenge*, 182.

22. It is difficult therefore to accept Cole's view that 'the socialism of Ernest Jones as it developed after 1848, was in its essentials that of Marx', *Socialist Thought*, 151.

23. G.J. Harney, 'To the working classes', *Democratic Review*, 1, 1849, 205.

24. E. Jones, 'Social right', *People's Paper*, 8 May 1852, in Saville, *Ernest Jones: Chartist*, 150; E. Jones, 'The law of supply and demand', *Notes to the People*, 1, 1851, 391.

25. E. Jones, 'Trades' grievances', ibid., 1, 1851, 422.

26. E. Jones, 'Introduction to the new world', ibid., 1, 1851, 134. Here there are certainly strong parallels with Marx and Engels' discussion of the same phenomenon in the *Communist Manifesto*, 84–5, where they write of 'the bourgeoisie ... doing away with the scattered state of the population, of the means of production and property. It has agglomerated population, centralized means of production, and has concentrated property in a few hands.'

27. E. Jones, 'The new world', *Notes to the People*, 1, 1851, 2; 'The Chartist programme', ibid., 1, 1851, 134.

28. E. Jones, 'The general good', ibid., 1, 1851, 244, 245.

29. E. Jones, 'Trades' grievances', ibid., 1, 1851, 342; 'Class war and class friendship', ibid., 2, 1852, 708, my emphasis.

30. E. Jones, 'Letters on the Chartist programme', ibid., 1, 1851, 84.

31. G.J. Harney. 'Letters of l'ami du peuple', *Red Republican*, 12 October 1850, 131.

32. Marx seems to have taken it from the French socialist Adolphe Blanqui, see N. Harding, 'Marx, Engels and the *Manifesto*: working class, party and proletariat', *Journal of Political Ideologies*, 3, 1998, 32–3.

33. E. Jones, 'The nationalisation of the land', *People's Paper*, June 1852 in Saville, *Ernest Jones: Chartist*, 153.

34. 'Programme', 259.

35. A. Plummer, 'The place of Bronterre O'Brien in the working-class movement', *Economic History Review*, 2, 1929–30, 75. O'Brien took from Ogilvie his tripartite categorisation of the value of land. See above Chapter 1.

36. 'Programme', 259.

37. E. Jones, 'Letters on the Chartist programme', *Notes to the People*, 1, 1851, 54.
38. E. Jones, 'The rival systems of agriculture', ibid., 1, 1851, 257, my emphasis.
39. H. Morton, *Red Republican*, 12 October 1850, 132.
40. On this see A, Hadfield, *The Chartist Land Company*, Newton Abbott: David and Charles, 1970.
41. J.B. O'Brien, *The Rise, Progress and Phases of Human Slavery*, London: 1885, 101, 144.
42. Quoted from A. Plummer, *Bronterre, a Political Biography of Bronterre O'Brien, 1804–64*, London: Allen and Unwin, 1971, 184.
43. H.V. Morton, 'Democratic organisations', *Red Republican*, 17 August 1850, 67.
44. E. Jones, 'Letters on the Chartist programme', *Notes to the People*, 1, 1851, 84, my emphasis.
45. 'Propositions of the National Reform League', in *Red Republican*, 17 August 1850, 68.
46. Jones, 'Social right', 151.
47. 'Programme', 261.
48. E. Jones, 'A letter to the advocates of the co-operative principle', *Notes to the People*, 1, 1851, 31; 'The national association of colliers and miners', ibid., 2, 1852, 560.
49. Jones, 'The general good', 246, my emphasis.
50. A friend and observer, 'Labor's grievances', ibid., 2, 1852, 1024; E. Jones, 'Trades' grievances', ibid., 1, 1851, 302; Jones, 'Letters on the Chartist programme', ibid., 84.
51. A friend, 'Labor's grievances', 1023. See here also proposition 2 of the National Reform League, *Red Republican*, 20 July 1850, 36. As regards the servicing of the National Debt this would henceforward be met by the proceeds of a property tax, while what was paid to fundholders would be deemed a repayment of principal rather than interest.
52. Jones, 'The co-operative movement', 587n.
53. In addition, as with Gray and Bray, the Chartist socialists saw the National Bank as playing an equilibrating role in the macroeconomy by matching aggregate purchasing power with the aggregate value of goods supplied. See proposition 7 of the National Reform League, *Red Republican*, 31 August 1850, 88.
54. O'Brien, *The Rise, Progress and Phases*, 139.
55. See *Red Republican*, 31 August 1850, 88.
56. 'Programme', 261.
57. Jones, 'The Chartist programme', 120, 131.
58. Schoyen, *The Chartist Challenge*, 197.
59. Saville, *Ernest Jones: Chartist*, 25.
60. Jones, 'The new world', 1; Jones, 'Letters on the Chartist programme', 73.

61. Jones, 'The new world', 1; *Bronterre's National Reformer*, 7 January 1837.
62. Saville, *Ernest Jones: Chartist*, 37.
63. Though, in this period, 'Owenism' did come 'increasingly to embrace more statist forms of social organisation', Claeys, *Citizens and Saints*, 262.
64. Editorial, 'Social and political reform', *Friend of the People*, 24 January 1851, 49.

Further Reading

Background

On changes in English agriculture in the eighteenth century and in particular the causes, extent and consequences of enclosure, see G.E. Mingay, *Parliamentary Enclosure in England, an Introduction to its Causes, Incidence and Impact, 1750–1850*, London: Longman, 1997; M. Turner, *Enclosure in Britain, 1750–1830*, London: Macmillan, 1984; and J. Chapman, 'The extent and nature of parliamentary enclosure', *Agricultural History Review*, 35, 1987, 25–35. As regards the consequences for the labourer, see in particular K. Snell, *Annals of the Labouring Poor: Social Change and Agrarian England, 1660–1900*, Cambridge: Cambridge University Press, 1985; and for the changing condition of the agricultural labourer in the late eighteenth and early nineteenth centuries, A. Armstrong, 'The position of the labourer in rural society', in G.E. Mingay (ed.), *The Agrarian History of England and Wales, 1750–1850*, Vol. 6, Cambridge: Cambridge University Press, 1989. On the impact of the wars on the distribution of agricultural income, see also G. Heuckel, 'English farming profits during the Napoleonic Wars, 1793–1815', *Explorations in Economic History*, 13, 1976, 331–45. As regards rural unrest in the period, see M. Reed, and R. Wells (eds), *Class, Conflict and Protest in the English Countryside, 1700–1880*, London: Frank Cass, 1990; also R. Wells, 'The development of the English rural proletariat and social protest, 1700–1850', *Journal of Peasant Studies*, 7, 1979, 115–39. For specific outbreaks of rural unrest, see A.J. Peacock, *Bread* or *Blood, a Study of the Agrarian Riots in East Anglia in 1816*, London: Gollancz, 1965; and E.J. Hobsbawm and G. Rudé, *Captain Swing*, Harmondsworth: Penguin, 1973.

For a discussion of the problem of public finance during the revolutionary and Napoleonic Wars, see P.K. O'Brien, 'Public finance in the wars with France, 1793–1815', in H.T. Dickinson (ed.), *Britain and the French Revolution*, London: Macmillan, 1989; C. Emsley, *British Society and the French Wars, 1793–1815*, London: Macmillan, 1979, considers the impact of these wars on British society; and P. Harling, *The Waning of 'Old Corruption', the Politics of Economical Reform in Britain, 1779–1846*, Oxford:

Clarendon Press, 1996 provides an excellent study of the retrenchment in government spending that spelt the end of Old Corruption.

On the industrial revolution an excellent general text is P. Hudson, *The Industrial Revolution*, London: Edward Arnold, 1992; see also N. Crafts, 'Industrial revolution', in R. Floud and D. McCloskey (eds), *The Economic History of Britain since 1700*, Vol. 1, 2nd edn, Cambridge: Cambridge University Press, 1994. For histories of the period which emphasise the gradual and incremental nature of economic change, see N. Crafts, *British Economic Growth during the Industrial Revolution*, Oxford: Oxford University Press, 1985; and E. Wrigley, *Continuity, Chance and Change: the Character of the Industrial Revolution in England*, Cambridge: Cambridge University Press, 1989. Some sense of changing perceptions of the industrial revolution in recent historiography can be had from P.K. O'Brien, 'Modern conceptions of the industrial revolution', in P.K. O'Brien and R. Quinault (eds), *The Industrial Revolution and British Society: Essays in Honour of Max Hartwell*, Cambridge: Cambridge University Press, 1993. For works that emphasise the profound nature of industrial and social changes which were occurring in the period see M. Berg, *The Age of Manufactures, 1700–1820, Industry, Innovation and Work in Britain*, 2nd edn, London:Routledge, 1994; and C. Behagg, *Politics and Production in Nineteenth Century England*, London: Routledge, 1990.

On the material condition of labour there is a vast literature, much of it revolving around the standard of living debate. One useful starting point here is A.J. Taylor, *The Standard of Living in the Industrial Revolution*, London: Methuen, 1975. But see also the general texts on the industrial revolution cited above; also P. Lindert, 'Unequal living standards', in Floud and McCloskey (eds), *The Economic History of Britain since 1700*, vol. 1. For a more general discussion of the condition and position of labour as England industrialised, see J. Belchem, *Industrialisation and the Working Class, the English Experience, 1750–1900*, Aldershot: Scolar, 1990.

For statistics on the growing importance of fixed capital investment, see C. Feinstein, and S. Pollard (eds), *Studies in Capital Formation in the United Kingdom, 1750–1920*, Oxford: Oxford University Press, 1988. But see also R. Samuel, 'The workshop of the world: steam power and hand technology in mid-Victorian Britain', *History Workshop Journal*, 3, 1977, 6–72 for a piece that emphasises the continuing and fundamental importance of labour power; also Berg, *The Age of Manufactures*. For studies of the changing size of industrial enterprises, see R. Lloyd-Jones and A.A. Le Roux, 'The size of firms in the cotton industry, Manchester, 1815–41', *Economic History Review*, 33, 1980, 72–82; V. Gatrell,

'Labour, power and the size of firms', *Economic History Review*, 30, 1977, 95–139; and again, *The Age of Manufactures*.

On class, class consciousness and the language of class there is an enormous literature, much of it produced in the last two decades. Three texts which may be used as a starting point here are C. Calhoun, *The Question of Class Struggle: Social Foundations of Popular Radicalism during the Industrial Revolution*, Oxford: Oxford University Press, 1982; G. Stedman Jones, *Languages of Class, Studies in Working-class History, 1832–1982*, Cambridge: Cambridge University Press, 1983; and P. Joyce, *Work, Society and Politics, the Culture of the Factory in Later Victorian England*, London: Methuen, 1982. For an antidote to Joyce and Jones, see N. Kirk, 'In defence of class: a critique of recent revisionist writing upon the nineteenth-century English working class', *International Review of Social History*, 32, 1987, 2–47. The debate engendered by these and other works can be followed in the volumes of *Social History* in the 1980s and 1990s.

Ideas

Chapter 1

For the basic texts see H.T. Dickinson, *The Collected Political Writings of Thomas Spence*, Newcastle upon Tyne: Avero, 1982; and M. Beer, *Pioneers of Land Reform*, London: Bell, 1920, which reprints William Ogilvie's *Essay on the Right of Property in Land* (1782).

M. Chase's *The People's Farm: English Radical Agrarianism, 1775–1840*, Oxford: Oxford University Press, 1988, furnishes the best discussion of the political economy of the agrarian radicals, but see also the early chapters of W. Stafford, *Socialism, Radicalism and Nostalgia: Social Criticism in Britain, 1775–1830*, Cambridge: Cambridge University Press, 1987. More specifically on the economic and political thought of Thomas Spence, see T. Knox, 'Thomas Spence: the trumpet of Jubilee', *Past and Present*, 76, 1977, 75–98; and T. Parsinnen's 'Thomas Spence and the origins of English land nationalization', *Journal of the History of Ideas*, 34, 1973, 135–41.

Accounts of Spence's life and thought can be found in P. Ashraf, *The Life and Times of Thomas Spence*, Newcastle upon Tyne: Graham, 1983 and O. Rudkin, *Thomas Spence and his Connections*, New York: Kelley, 1966.

Chapter 2

For the primary texts, see N. Thompson and D. Eastwood (eds), *The Collected Social and Political Writings of William Cobbett*, 16

vols, London: Routledge/Thoemmes, 1998. For a full descriptive
bibliography of Cobbett's writings, see M. Pearl, *William Cobbett,
a Bibliographical Account of his Life and Times*, Oxford: Oxford
University Press, 1953.

On Cobbett's thought, see I. Dyck, *William Cobbett and Rural
Popular Culture*, Cambridge: Cambridge University Press, 1992;
L. Nattrass, *William Cobbett, the Politics of Style*, Cambridge:
Cambridge University Press, 1995; and R. Williams, *Cobbett*,
Oxford: Oxford University Press, 1983. There is a fascinating
discussion of the nature of the language used by Cobbett and also
Spence in O. Smith, *The Politics of Language, 1791–1819*, Oxford:
Clarendon Press, 1984. An interesting study of Cobbett in
relation to radical thought and radical politics in the Napoleonic
Wars period can be found in P. Spence, *The Birth of Romantic
Radicalism, War, Popular Politics and English Radical Reformism,
1800–1815*, Aldershot: Scolar, 1996. Two excellent, though very
different, biographies of Cobbett are D. Green's, *Great Cobbett,
the Noblest Agitator*, Oxford: Oxford University Press, 1985; and
G. Spater, *William Cobbett, the Poor Man's Friend*, 2 vols,
Cambridge: Cambridge University Press, 1982.

Chapter 4

Many of the primary texts cited in this chapter can be found in K.
Carpenter (ed.) *The Framework Knitters and Handloom Weavers*,
New York: Arno, 1972; and K. Carpenter (ed.), *The Spitalfields
Acts, Seven Pamphlets*, New York: Arno, 1972; but see also G.
Henson's *A History of the Framework Knitters*, Leicester: 1831. *The
First and Second Reports from the Select Committee on the Petitions of
the Ribbon Weavers* [1818], reprinted by the Irish University Press,
1976 provides a fascinating insight into the economic and ethical
arguments deployed by those who sought and those who opposed
the legislative buttressing of a moral economy.

On the moral economy tradition see E.P. Thompson, 'The
moral economy of the English crowd in the eighteenth century',
Past and Present, 50, 1971, 76–136; and *The Making of the English
Working Class*, Harmondsworth: Penguin, 1975, 259–346. See
also E.J. Hobsbawm, 'Custom, wages and workload in nineteenth-century industry', in *Labouring Men, Studies in the History
of Labour*, London: Weidenfeld and Nicolson, 1964; I. Prothero,
*Artisans and Politics in Early Nineteenth-century London, John Gast
and his Times*, Folkestone: Dawson, 1979, in particular Parts 1
and 3; and A.J. Randall, *Before the Luddites: Custom, Community
and Machinery in the English Woollen Industry, 1776–1809*,
Cambridge: Cambridge University Press, 1991. For the moral
discourse of labour in the later nineteenth century, see P. Joyce,

Visions of the People, Industrial England and the Question of Class,
Cambridge: Cambridge University Press, 1991.

Chapter 5

As regards the primary texts Hodgskin's *Labour Defended against
the Claims of Capital,* 1825, his *Popular Political Economy,* 1827
and his *The Natural and Artificial Rights of Property Contrasted,*
1832 have all been reprinted by Augustus Kelley.
    Until recently the only substantial assessment of Thomas
Hodgskin's life and thought was that of E. Halévy, *Thomas
Hodgskin,* translated with an introduction by A.J. Taylor,
London: Benn, 1956. However, D. Stack's, *Nature and Artifice,
the Life and Thought of Thomas Hodgskin, 1787–1869,* London:
Royal Historical Society, Boydell and Brewer, 1998, now
provides the definitive study. Marx's evaluation of Hodgskin can
be found in Volume 3 of his *Theories of Surplus Value,* London:
Lawrence and Wishart, 1972. For a discussion of Hodgskin's
relation to Marx, see E.K. Hunt, 'Value theory in the writings of
the classical economists, Thomas Hodgskin and Karl Marx',
History of Political Economy, 9, 1977, 323–45 and, for a consideration of his critique of classical political economy, see J. Jaffe,
'The origins of Thomas Hodgskin's critique of political
economy', *History of Political Economy,* 27, 1995, 493–515.

Chapter 6

As to primary texts the major works of Robert Owen are to be
found in G. Claeys (ed.), *Selected Works of Robert Owen,* 4 vols,
London: Pickering, 1993. William Thompson's *An Inquiry into
the Principles of the Distribution of Wealth,* 1824 and his *Labor
Rewarded,* 1827, have been reprinted by Augustus Kelley.
    On early nineteenth-century socialist political economy, see G.
Claeys, *Citizens and Saints: Politics and Anti-politics in Early British
Socialism,* Cambridge: Cambridge University Press, 1989 and his
*Machinery, Money and the Millennium, from Moral Economy to
Economic Socialism, 1815–60,* London: Polity, 1987. Also excel-
lent is W. Stafford's *Socialism, Radicalism and Nostalgia: Social
Criticism in Britain, 1775–1830.* See also N. Thompson's *The
Market and its Critics, Socialist Political Economy in Nineteenth
Century Britain,* London: Routledge, 1988; and G.D.H. Cole's
Socialist Thought, the Forerunners, 1789–1850, London:
Macmillan, 1959 is still worth a look. Also on Owen and, more
generally, early nineteenth-century communitarian socialism, see
R.G. Garnett, *Co-operation and the Owenite Socialist Communities
in Britain, 1825–45,* Manchester: Manchester University Press,

1972; and J.F.C. Harrison, *Robert Owen and the Owenites in Britain and America, the Quest for the New Moral World*, London: Routledge and Kegan Paul, 1969. More specifically on Thompson's value theory, see E.K. Hunt, 'Utilitarianism and the labour theory of value: a critique of the ideas of William Thompson', *History of Political Economy*, 11, 1979, 545–71.

As for biographies see R.K.P. Pankhurst, *William Thompson, 1775–1833, Pioneer Socialist*, London: Pluto, 1991; and for Owen, G.D.H. Cole, *The Life of Robert Owen*, 3rd edn, London: Frank Cass, 1965.

Chapter 7

There have been reprints of many of these papers, but see in particular those of the *Pioneer*, 1833–34 and the *Crisis*, 1832–34 by Greenwood Press.

On the working-class press and its popularisation of political economy, see P. Hollis, *The Pauper Press, a Study in Working-class Radicalism in the 1830s*, Oxford: Oxford University Press, 1970; and N. Thompson, *The People's Science, the Popular Political Economy of Exploitation and Crisis, 1816–34*, Cambridge: Cambridge University Press, 1984.

On the trade unionism of the early 1830s, see G.D.H. Cole, *Attempts at General Union, a Study in British Trade Union History, 1818–34*, London: Macmillan, 1953; W. Oliver, 'The Consolidated Trades' Union of 1834', *Economic History Review*, 17, 1965, 77–95; the articles by Sykes and Fryson in J. Rule (ed.), *British Trade Unionism, 1750–1850, the Formative Years*, London: Longman, 1988; and the more narrowly focused pieces by M.J. Haynes, 'Class and class conflict in the early nineteenth century: Northampton shoemakers and the Grand National Consolidated Trades' Union', *Literature and History*, 5, 1977, 73–94; and T. Parsinnen and I. Prothero, 'The London tailors' strike of 1834 and the collapse of the Grand National Consolidated Trades' Union, a police spy's report', *International Review of Social History*, 22, 1977, 65–107.

Chapter 8

J.F. Bray's *Labour's Wrongs*, 1839, John Gray's *Lecture on Human Happiness*, 1825, *The Social System*, 1831, *An Efficient Remedy for the Distress of Nations*, 1842 and his *Lectures on the Nature and Use of Money*, 1848 have all been reprinted by Augustus Kelley. M. Jolliffe, 'John Francis Bray', *International Review for Social History*, 4, 1939, 1–36, reprints many of Bray's letters which were published in American papers.

Specifically on the political economy of Gray and Bray, see J. Kimball, *The Economic Doctrines of John Gray, 1799-1883*, Washington: Catholic University of America, 1946; J. Henderson, 'An English communist Mr. Bray [and] his remarkable work', *History of Political Economy*, 17, 1985, 73–95; and H.J. Carr, 'The social and political thought of John Francis Bray', unpublished PhD thesis, University of London, 1942.

More generally on the nature of the political economy of Bray, Gray and other early nineteenth-century British socialist writers, see J. King, 'Utopian or scientific? A reconsideration of the Ricardian socialists', *History of Political Economy*, 15, 1983, 345–73; while on their relationship to Marx, see E.K. Hunt, 'The relation of the Ricardian socialists to Ricardo and Marx', *Science and Society*, 44, 1980, 177–98.

A short biographical piece on Bray by Carr is to be found in *Economica*, 7, 1940, 397–514; and D. Martin and J. Saville, 'John Francis Bray, 1809–97, radical reformer and Owenite', in J. Saville and J. Bellamy (eds), *Dictionary of Labour Biography*, Vol. 3, London: Macmillan, 1976, 21–5. For Gray, see D. Martin, 'John Gray, early socialist and currency reformer, 1799–1883' in J. Bellamy and J. Saville (eds), *Dictionary of Labour Biography*, Vol. 6, London: Macmillan, 1982, 121–5.

Chapter 9

As to primary texts in addition to the Merlin reprint of the *Red Republican* there have also been reprints of Ernest Jones' *Notes to the People*, Merlin Press, George Harney's *Democratic Review*, Barnes and Noble, and his *Friend of the people*, Merlin Press.

On the political economy of the Chartist socialists, see J. Saville's excellent introductions to *Ernest Jones: Chartist*, London: Lawrence and Wishart, 1952; and the Merlin Press reprint of the *Red Republican*. See also good short discussions in D.J.V. Jones, *Chartism and the Chartists*, London: Allen Lane, 1975; and E. Royle, *Chartism*, 3rd edn, London: Longman, 1996. For the relation of the Chartists to trade unionism in this period, see J. Belchem, 'Chartism and the trades, 1848–50', *English Historical Review*, 98, 1983, 558–87.

For biographical studies of Harney, Jones and O'Brien, see A. Schoyen, *The Chartist Challenge: a Portrait of George Julian Harney*, London: Heinemann, 1958; A. Plummer, *Bronterre: a Political Biography of Bronterre O'Brien, 1804–64*, London: Allen and Unwin, 1971; and Saville, *Ernest Jones: Chartist*.

Index

agrarian radicalism *see* Ogilvie; Spence
agriculture, dominance of, 1, 11, 18–19, 29, 77, 128
Amiens, Peace of (1802), 23
Anti-Corn Law League, 56
apprenticeships, 31–2, 37, 141nn
artisans, 30, 31, 79, 131
Assize of Bread, abolished, 34
Association for the Preservation of Liberty and Property, 14

Bank of England, 24–5, 26
banks: labour, 74, 81, 89; proposed National, 99–100, 108–9, 117, 125, 155n
Bentham, Jeremy, 45, 63–4
Birmingham, 32; Equitable Labour Exchange, 74
Black, John, 63
Blanc, Louis, *ateliers nationaux*, 113, 116–17
Blatchford, Robert, 43
Boards of Trade, 42, 108–9
Boon, M.J., 128
Bowring, John, 63–4
Bray, John Francis, 83, 84, 101, 102, 117, 131, 132; analysis of exploitation, 104–7, 133; joint stock enterprises, 107–8; *Labour's Wrongs*, 102, 107, 151n; socialist commonwealth, 109–10
British Association for the Promotion of Co-operative Knowledge, 14, 74

capital: centralisation of, 119; derived from labour, 84–5, 104–5; distribution of, 65–6; fixed and circulating, 48–9, 83; power of, 40, 47–8, 133–4

capitalism, and class antagonism, 36, 49–51
capitalists, 101, 105; attitude to labour, 71–2, 87–8, 144n; exploitation by, 49–50, 52–3, 55, 133
Chalmers, George, 24
Chartism, 57, 116–17, 128–9, 132; class antagonism in, 119–20, 129–30; Land Plan, 121; legacy of, 127–8; nation-alisation, 120–2; socialist political economy, 112–14, 117–18, 129–30
Chartist Convention (1851), 112, 120
child labour, 31
class, analysis of, 36, 47, 49
class antagonism, 3–4, 62, 143n; in Chartism, 119–20, 129–30; and exploitation, 49–51, 52–3, 105–6; and industrialisation, 35–6, 133–4; and political radicalism, 81, 87; in Thompson, 66, 71–2
classical economics, 43, 46, 55, 67, 95
co-operative communities: Owen's, 60–1, 62–3, 68; Thompson's, 72–3
co-operatives: experimental, 73–4, 100–1, 111, 115–16; producer, 122–4, 127, 128–9; trade unions and, 80–1
Cobbett, William, 20–1, 26–7; antipathy to industrialisation, 28–9; 'Old Corruption', 24–6, 46, 49, 129, 131; *Perish Commerce!*, 28–9; political economy, 25–9, 133
collective ownership: means of production, 12–13, 84, 92,

*Index compiled by
Auriol Griffith-Jones*